it differ from communism? The author of this book contends that socialism as well as the doctrine of free enterprise can be democratic, but that communism cannot; that communism is "the theory and practice of totalitarian power by a comparatively small, deeply intrenched government bureaucracy."

In a final chapter Mr. Biddle asks whether our government, changed but little since 1787, can function effectively in its new tremendous role. He concludes that we have inherited a provincial and parochial point of view, normal to our federal traditions, but not calculated to express an international, or even a national, outlook.

MR. BIDDLE *was Attorney General of the United States during World War II and American member of the International Military Tribunal which tried the principal German war criminals.*

This book has grown out of a Walgreen lecture series at The University of Chicago.

THE WORLD'S BEST HOPE

If there be any among us who would wish to dissolve this Union or to change its republican form, let them stand undisturbed as monuments of the safety with which error of opinion may be tolerated where reason is left free to combat it. I know, indeed, that some honest men fear that a republican government can not be strong, that this government is not strong enough; but would the honest patriot, in the full tide of successful experiment, abandon a government which has so far kept us free and firm on the theoretic and visionary fear that this Government, the world's best hope, may by possibility want energy to preserve itself? I trust not. I believe this, on the contrary, the strongest Government on earth.

THOMAS JEFFERSON
First Inaugural Address, March 4, 1801

THE WORLD'S BEST HOPE

A Discussion
of the Role of the United States
in the Modern World

BY FRANCIS BIDDLE

THE UNIVERSITY OF CHICAGO PRESS
CHICAGO · ILLINOIS

CHARLES R. WALGREEN FOUNDATION LECTURES

F °G 5
.B4-7

THE UNIVERSITY OF CHICAGO PRESS, CHICAGO 37
Cambridge University Press, London, N.W. 1, England
W. J. Gage & Co., Limited, Toronto 2B, Canada

For

MARY WINSLOW

with

GRATITUDE AND AFFECTION

AUTHOR'S NOTE

☼

THIS book is based on a course of lectures delivered, at the invitation of the Charles R. Walgreen Foundation for the Study of American Institutions, at the University of Chicago in February, 1948. It deals largely with the flow of current affairs in a far from static world. But, although history constantly changes, the problems which underlie it keep reasserting themselves. It has, therefore, seemed to me worth while to separate some of these problems from the confusion of hurrying events and to try to analyze their significance.

FRANCIS BIDDLE

WASHINGTON, D.C.
August 1948

INTRODUCTION

✻

AMERICANS are today a deeply puzzled and not too happy people. The rush of events in the three years that followed the war has carried the necessity for decisions which they were not prepared to make. Tendencies which had been developing since World War I, but which had been hardly noticed and never fully realized, suddenly became accomplished facts. Of these, the most significant is the disappearance of Great Britain as the political and economic center of a world which she had held together for a hundred years of relative peace, between Waterloo and Sarajevo. Now there is no longer that centripetal force. History, like physics, abhors a vacuum. For over thirty years the power that was Great Britain's had been gradually ebbing. Yet the immense importance of this change did not generally become apparent until the spring of 1947.

Who was to fill the vacuum?

The United States had emerged, after World War I, as the chief banking and creditor nation of the world. Today she is the "great power house of the world with two-thirds of the manufactures and three-quarters of the investments."[1] She alone produces a surplus far greater than her needs. But her political strength as an agent of peace is untested and largely unknown. Unlike Britain a hundred years ago, she does not operate in the open area of free trade but, on one side of the ocean, in an immense domestic market until recently protected by a tariff wall; and abroad, rather at arm's length, with a group of nations divided by tariff barriers and trade restrictions and incapable of producing enough exports, after the destruction and dislocation of a second world war, to pay for the imports, chiefly from America, which they must have. Russia, undeveloped industrially, immensely rich in all natural resources, with the compact yet flexible political system of the modern totalitarian state, dominating the tight group of the satellite countries, pushes steadily her imperialism where any weak spot is found and apparently waits for the breakdown of capitalism to open further opportunities.

To Americans the new shift of power was not clear immediately after the war. It was not until the end of February, 1947, that we began to realize what that shift meant in terms of American responsibility which circumstances, with apparent suddenness, had forced on our surprised consciousness. It was inevitable that the pull of the vacuum in Greece should have led us so quickly to consider the vaster emptiness of all Europe. Yet we were unprepared for the speed and insistence with which the transfer of power was forcing us into a central position of authority of which we had not dreamed and which we did not want. We had lived in a state of adolescence in which the possession of power did not seem to involve responsibility. We had enjoyed, increasingly since the Spanish-American War, the exciting sense of the first without the sobering realization of the second. We had had our cake and eaten it too.

But now all at once we had come of age, had graduated into a world of adults, where we were expected to play a part which we had always assumed had been and would be allotted to others by a wise and friendly Providence. It was all very well to comfort ourselves, even before the end of the war, by the pleasing reflection that we had abandoned our doctrine of isolation by helping to organize the United Nations. The American passion for moral decisions spread on legal paper lulled vague worries about the future into an optimistic feeling of accomplishment. To most of us the new commitments meant formulas that could be neatly decided by national votes in the international field—we still believed that it was peopled by men of good will, like ourselves—so as to permit a return to that other real world of domestic normalcy. We did not conceive what a different place it would prove to be in the running of a few brief years.

The announcement by Secretary Marshall in June, 1947, of the new plan to help Europe cut away what was left of the comfort of isolation. As the months went by, and we thought about this novel conception, we began unhappily to realize that we were being asked to abandon our separateness from Europe not only as a theoretic policy but as an actual way of living. It meant not merely sitting around a peace table but dealing, as England had so long dealt, with the infinitely complicated problems which had never before concerned us. We were expected no longer to make moral judgments about other countries from the pure heights of our isolation but to take decisions that involved action. Greece, on the sidelines, held together by British troops in 1944–45, was a different matter from the empty Greece of 1947. We could talk about a hundred thousand Jews a month entering Palestine. Could we act when the time for action came?

In our hearts rose the nostalgia of the America we had known, untouched by these problems, which had alighted on us so suddenly and roosted, like lean and watching vultures, at the foot of our comfortable beds. We no longer felt that our world "was a safe place, watched over by a kindly God, who exacted nothing but cheerfulness and good-will from his children; and the American flag was a sort of rainbow in the sky, promising that all storms were over."[2] We were deeply disturbed by the abrupt ending of the daydreams of our youth.

At the same time we cannot enjoy the good things of the peace for which we had longed for four years. It is not comfortable to know that the people from whom we had sprung, really our own people, were cold and starving. The contrast haunts us. If the world is indeed one, as we had heard, would our prosperity last while their poverty increased? Was our safe American world gone forever? . . . We cannot see this strange world ahead of us.

Policies, whether they are domestic or international, are evolved empirically, from the conflicting tug of daily events. The European Recovery Plan grew out of a realization of the direction of events in Europe and will be further shaped by the outcome of future events. It is based, however, on one or two general principles. One of these is that we propose to help countries of Europe revive their economy "so as to permit the emergence of political and social conditions in which free institutions can exist." If this assumption is intrinsic to the program—and it would now appear to be pretty clear that we do not propose to help countries which are endeavoring to suppress democratic institutions—it becomes pertinent to inquire what those institutions mean to Americans. Is laissez faire, for instance, one of them? But that inquiry, in view of our new relationship to those other countries which are to join us in this great effort, does not go far enough. We must ask, further, what Europeans mean by democratic institutions. We shall find, I venture to think, that in some fields there will be agreement, not in others. Accordingly, the last determination will be whether there is a sufficient area of agreement within which this doctrine of European recovery can be applied.

Put differently, and less theoretically, can the system of free enterprise of the United States be made to work in harmony with the Socialist or semi-Socialist governments of western Europe in an effort to rebuild the economy and sustain the free political and social cultures of those countries?

These questions I propose to examine in the following pages.

CONTENTS

I

THIS YEAR OF GRACE

✻

WHAT is the place of the United States in the world in this Year of Grace 1948? The prosperity of the American people, immediately after a war into which we had poured three hundred billion dollars, defines an aspect of our new position—physical power. Its significance is sharpened by the contrast with all other peoples.

Our material life, compared even with the fullest living of our own past, let alone European standards, shows an expansion and distribution of satisfactions which, a few years ago, the more optimistic economists hardly dared to outline as a goal. What would have sounded in 1938 like a "silly" utopian dream to the more conservative or skeptical is now a reality. With extraordinary ease our reconversion followed an all-out war of destruction. We had built up a titanic war machine—a whole nation geared to war. How, without serious interruptions, could we build back the peace machine? In 1944 and 1945 the pile of surplus war goods hung over the horizon of victory, a serious impediment that might be expected to dislocate the flow back to our peace economy and upset the mechanism of prices in a market always sensitive to clouds or, at least, always thought to be so. Counsel in the government was divided between those who suggested that planning for the decontrol period was lagging behind the sudden rush of the future, when Germany or Japan would collapse, and the others who said no, we must not theorize or blueprint now; the war effort would suffer from premature patterns of reconversion; there would yet be time. Some prophets of the immediate future—who could or wished to see beyond a few years?—foretold that vast unemployment would follow war, certainly if government controls were removed with too much speed, and insisted that the country must prepare comprehensive plans for public works to take up the slack while production for war was being changed back to production for peace and while millions of war veterans looked for immediate employment. Meanwhile private industry planned, blueprinted, and, when the time came, promptly retooled.

The prophecies of unemployment were not realized. Not only was the immense readjustment from war to peace carried out with an easy, smooth, almost casual ease, as if we took it in our quiet stride, without making too much of it, but the huge body of soldiers and sailors was at the same time reabsorbed into the complex machine of industry while it was being readapted to receive them.

A group of economists, associated with J. Frederic Dewhurst, of the Twentieth Century Fund, which authorized and underwrote the study, took the measure of our entire economy, projecting it into estimates for 1950 and 1960, in a volume published in 1947 under the title *America's Needs and Resources*. They found that extraordinary flexibility had been learned under the stimulating impact of war, when it was discovered that productive capacity could be enlarged without creating new capital equipment. Small changes in machinery made it easy to shift from one product to another. "Shifts of this sort were made from food machinery to amphibious tanks, from typewriters to small parts for guns, from printing presses to machine tools, from refrigerators to marine engines and helicopters." This flexibility characterized the readjustment to peacetime requirements. It was an amazing feat. "During the war we increased our manufacturing facilities— though in a distorted fashion—by roughly 50 per cent. We were able to expand our productive capacity enormously and rapidly, devote almost half our economic effort to production for war, and still maintain a high living standard for the civilian population." And our economists, filling in the extravagant picture with minute detail of chart and graph, wrote: "We have more than enough manpower and resources and potential productive facilities to fulfill our requirements under every conceivable circumstance. Fears of excess capacity need not trouble us unduly."[1]

"Americans," commented David Cushman Coyle, reviewing this study, "are supposed to be a boastful race, but America in the twentieth century has probably suffered more from underestimation than from any other illusion. . . . If the United States does not get into an atomic war or a serious depression; and if our growth, technology, and habits go on along their present lines, we can expect to produce more on a peace-time schedule of about thirty-eight hours a week in 1960 than we put out in 1944 at the war-time peak at forty-seven hours a week."[2]

In an incredibly short period we had refashioned the mighty plant we had created for war, holding the stream of production, now to be used, we assumed, almost altogether to satisfy the needs of a world at peace. There was substantially no unemployment. Scarcity of manpower continued, and wages advanced during the readjustment about on a par with the advance of prices. Production constantly increased. In the second year after the war was over it reached the highest level of any peace year in the history of the country.

But the study revealed another side of the picture. "The real dangers are an inadequate level of income and a low standard of living." It found the housing situation far from satisfactory. In 1940, of the thirty-seven million dwelling units, sixteen million needed to be replaced or rehabilitated. About 30 per cent had no running water, 40 per cent no flush toilet, 45 per cent no private bath or shower. For the same year about two-thirds of all farmhouses were substandard. Nearly 29 per cent of the dwelling units in metropolitan districts were located in blighted areas.[3] There is, no doubt, less crowding and more use of modern "comforts" than in Europe. But the test does not lie in such a comparison but in determining the extent to which our immense productive achievements have been translated into a corresponding level of consumption.

The unnecessary housing shortage today; the cost of building well out of reach of the average pocketbook; the archaic jumble of outdated housing codes; the absurd labor-union regulations (painters may use only a certain size brush); the "sticky" practices of the building industry; the timidity and uncertainty of the government program; the greedy and unimaginative resistance of the real estate interests to the development of any adequate government low-cost housing program —all these things exist now as they existed at the end of the war. We have hardly made an effort to solve the housing problem.

Meanwhile the cost of living rises with ruthless precision. Apparently on the theory that the "temporary" inflation, which was to be expected until we were fully back in production again, could best be checked by giving a generous opportunity for the law of supply and demand to operate freely, we gaily tossed controls overboard. The law worked all right. Prices went up and continue their inevitable ascent.

One other conclusion of the Twentieth Century Fund study must be taken into consideration to complete this brief glance at our economic resources and requirements—a conclusion which has a definite bearing on the development of our future foreign policy. Examining our natural resources, the authors of the study find that some of the most valuable are "likely to become deficient in one or two decades. . . . Supplies of most of our high-grade metallic ores are in this class. The known zinc, lead and bauxite reserves that are now commercially feasible to utilize will be exhausted by 1960''; crude petroleum and natural gas probably not for another twenty years. The economists therefore recommend the development of "a policy of freely relying on imports to the extent that they are necessary to compensate for deficiencies in domestic sources.''[4]

A large part of the community in those days that immediately followed the cessation of hostilities was deeply concerned with the future of the labor movement. Labor, or at least many labor leaders, had, it was believed, grown undisciplined, dictatorial, often violent, and sometimes corrupt; labor practices were undemocratic and frequently despotic; labor had been "coddled" too long by the prophets of the New Deal, particularly during the war, and needed curbing. It was insisted that legislation to carry out these views be enacted if some balance of forces was to be restored. On the other hand, it was urged that a free labor movement represented one of the essentials to insure against the "Fascist menace" within our country. Our prosperity demanded that the organized labor movement, which had grown in rough numbers from three or four to fifteen million in the dozen years before our entrance into the war, be not checked or broken in the inevitable back-to-normalcy swing. And what about wages? Could labor hold the real wages which the manpower shortage during the war had afforded an opportunity to increase and sustain? Was collective bargaining, so slowly achieved, to be scrapped?

There had been sporadic strikes (with one or two more serious exceptions) during the war, as there were indeed in England, as was to be expected from a people not nurtured on controls. On the whole, labor and management went along with directives of the War Labor Board. When the wave of

strikes broke out in 1946, a nervous public began to fear that
they would not get the washing machines, automobiles,
radios, electric toasters, and the other "necessities" of which
the war had temporarily deprived them. How long was this
sort of thing to keep up? Why couldn't everyone get together
and produce? Were these horrid dislocations, from which it
was difficult to see how the "public" ever got anything, going
to continue, to increase—a wasteful, permanent destructive
power, born perhaps out of the thinking of Karl Marx? Could
it be stopped by law?

The strikes rose and fell and swept the country. Labor blew
off steam with a vengeance—so much had accumulated during
the war. Perhaps that was inevitable; to try its own strength,
to test its discipline, to show it could fight if it had to, to hit
first, to assert its independence. That, after all, was the traditional American way.

Then came the congressional elections, the Taft-Hartley
Act, and, well before its passage, the tapering-off of strikes, as
the steam was temporarily exhausted.

So much for our domestic economy since the firing ceased.
In the foreign field there was a complete reversal in our relation to foreign countries in less than three years.

If we look back over our brief history as a nation, starting
with the warnings of the Founding Fathers against precisely
what we are now doing, we can more vividly realize how
radical is the change in the most fundamental of all American
foreign policies. Even before Washington had delivered his
eloquent and wise Farewell Address on September 17, 1796,
others had warned their countrymen to be independent of
Europe. Isolation in foreign policy, as Samuel E. Morison
has suggested, was a natural result of the isolation of pioneer
communities. In 1775 John Adams remarked: "We ought to
lay it down as a first principle, and maxim never to be for-

gotten, to maintain an entire neutrality in all future European wars." The year the Declaration was signed Thomas Paine, in *Common Sense*, warned against dependence on Great Britain which tended to involve us in European wars and quarrels. "As Europe is our market for trade, we ought to form no partial connection with any part of it. It is the true interest of America to steer clear of European contentions." Nine years later Dr. Richard Price begged his countrymen to avoid connections with Europe. "Why should they . . . expose themselves to the danger of being involved in its quarrels? . . . Indeed, I tremble when I think of that rage for trade which is likely to prevail among them."[5]

But the "rage for trade" was ever stronger than the desire to keep clear of the Old World, from which Americans believed they had forever escaped; and trade we did on all the seven seas, breaking all transatlantic sailing records—twelve and a quarter days from Boston to Liverpool—with our clipper ships: "*Nightingale* and *Witch of the Wave*, *Northern Light* and *Southern Cross*, *Young America* and *Great Republic*, *Golden Age* and *Herald of the Morning*, *Red Jacket* and *Westward Ho!*, *Dreadnought* and *Glory of the Seas*."[6] The young democracy might wish to avoid entangling alliances, but she would not give up her foreign trade for a theory and, being young, need not be consistent. She could have her cake and eat it, after the preliminary tangles with Britain, because she could count on Britain's navy to keep open the channels of the sea.

Washington thought that we could have commercial without political foreign relations, saying in his Farewell Address to the American people: "The Great rule of conduct for us, in regard to foreign Nations is in extending our commercial relations to have with them as little *political* connection as possible. . . . Europe has a set of primary interests, which to us have none, or a very remote relation. . . . Our detached and distant situation invites and enables us to pursue a different course. . . . Why, by interweaving our destiny with that of any part of Europe, entangle our peace and prosperity in the toils of European Ambition, Rivalship, Interest, Humor or Caprice." A generation later Jefferson added: "Our first and fundamental maxim should be, never to entangle ourselves in the broils of Europe."

In 1835 Alexis de Tocqueville, who understood so profoundly the America of his day, wrote: "The policy of the Americans in relation to the whole world is exceedingly simple; and it may almost be said that nobody stands in need of them, nor do they stand in need of anybody. Their independence is never threatened. . . . As the Union takes no part in the affairs of Europe, it has, properly speaking, no foreign interests to discuss."[7]

Some fifty years later James Bryce noted: "In foreign policy, where the need for continuity is greatest, the United States has little to do . . . the problems . . . are far fewer and usually far simpler than those of the Old World . . . and the likelihood from any danger from abroad is so slender that it may be practically ignored. . . . America has little occasion to think of foreign affairs. . . . There is a determination in all classes to keep European interference at a distance." He concluded that, finally, "absolute neutrality and impartiality as regards the Old World is observed," giving as a striking example of this attitude our delay and hesitation before we ratified the Brussels International Slave Trade Act in 1892. We are at this very moment of our history more sharply aware than ever of the unfortunate results of such an attitude which Bryce characterized as the ignorance of foreign affairs of our leading statesmen, inducing carelessness in the choice of persons to represent us abroad, the discontinuity of policy, and the difficulty of handling issues with promptness and success. Some of these difficulties I shall have occasion to discuss in a subsequent chapter. In other respects Bryce thought our detachment "an unspeakable blessing,*' chiefly because no army was needed, except to repress Indian troubles, by a nation "extremely jealous of a standing army."[8]

The scope and suddenness of the change are illustrated by a brief review of what occurred after the first World War and by comparing the two periods. Then, too, our allies—France, England, Russia, with the United States—had won an exhausting victory over the Central Powers. Then, too, the United States, which had come late into the fighting but whose incredible power had concluded it, emerged with her industrial resources unscathed—immensely, in fact, enlarged and expanded under the war effort. After the second war she was even more the acknowledged creditor and lending nation of the world, as England had been for over a hundred years. Europe was now more desperately in need than ever; its economy, shattered in 1914–18, was now toppling, and it was looking to us as the only possible source of material aid.

Yet there were several striking differences when we compare 1945–47 with 1918–20. Even before the second World War was over, the great and little powers had agreed on a mechanism which, it was hoped, might be used to settle peacefully the struggles which hitherto had brought about war. Apparently the United States considered herself no longer isolated. This time we led the world in organizing the new order. We were as integral a member of the United Nations as any other—a circumstance dramatized by the selection of New York as the permanent seat for the international deliberations. The International Bank, with an American president, was created and slowly began to function.

Perhaps the most hopeful practical step toward a deeper and more effective world co-operation was taken when representatives of twenty-three nations negotiated a tentative Trade Agreements Act at Geneva, Switzerland, calculated to prevent the repetition of the high tariffs, empire preferences, and other protective practices which, twenty-five years before, had dammed up the natural flow of international trade. Our country, represented by William L. Clayton, Undersecretary of State for Foreign Affairs—patient, practical, and never losing sight of his goal—took the lead to bring about a condition which approached free trade among the nations.

This American attitude represented a profound alteration in national policy to fit the changed circumstances. The United States, now consciously a creditor nation, was beginning to adopt the historic free-trade role of Great Britain by throwing her influence against international restrictions. A line was drawn, it is true, between tariffs, which were permitted, and quotas and import restrictions, which were conditionally forbidden. The approach, foreshadowed in reciprocal trade agreements, was a complete change in our thinking after World War I. We matched our insistence to foreign countries that they let down the bars by actually lowering our own duties on many articles. To what extent this give-and-take will be continued is on the knees of the congressional gods. But it would seem that we have begun to realize that it must be a condition to any foreign trade. The pressure of the United States for a freer world economy had begun well before the program for the recovery of Europe was launched and fitted logically with the Marshall Plan as it developed. This relation found expression in Mr. Clayton's presence at the discussions of the sixteen European nations in Paris, which finally led to the report, on September 22, 1947, of the Committee of European Economic Co-operation. On September 10 Mr. Clayton stated: "If we cannot reduce the barriers to world trade and thus make possible a great expansion in the production, distribution, and consumption of goods throughout the world, there is little hope that any aid we may extend under the Marshall proposal will accomplish its purpose or be more than a stop-gap measure."[9]

While Molotov was in London resisting all efforts to achieve a settlement in Germany, rising to new heights of invective and the endless delay of obstinacy, the United States Senate, by a vote of 72 to 1, ratified the Inter-American Treaty of Reciprocal Assistance. Experience in the United Nations might have discouraged a similar effort, though limited to the Western Hemisphere. But the Defense Treaty went much further than the United Nations Charter, perhaps because of what its signatories had learned from that experience. The treaty, remarked Senator Vandenberg, contained no "paralyzing veto" on mutual efforts to keep the peace. Controversies are to be submitted to peaceful settlement; an armed attack from within or without the hemisphere is "considered an attack against all the American states," and they are committed, under a two-thirds vote, to take joint action. The only exception is that each state may reserve the right not to participate in military operations. The treaty reaffirms the principles of the Monroe Doctrine and expands the doctrine by making the defense of this hemisphere not the self-imposed obligation of the United States but the responsibility of all the American republics.

But the Senate did not confine the participation of this country in military alliances to the Western Hemisphere. On May 19, 1948, the Foreign Relations Committee unanimously recommended, and on June 10 the Senate by a vote of 64 to 4 adopted, a resolution which, among other things, expressed the sense of the Senate that our government pursue as an objective: "Association of the United States by constitutional process with such regional and other collective arrangements as are based on continuous and effective self-help and mutual aid, and as affect its national security."[10] This meant military help to international alliances, a far-reaching development of our increasing responsibilities.

The history of 1919 was not repeating itself.

Gone is our physical isolation, our geographical separation from the matrix of Europe. The once wide ocean between us has shrunk under the impact of radio and airplane. The Atlantic no longer separates and is no longer a defense to a sheltered America. We tried "absolute neutrality" in the first great modern war of the world and again in the second. We found each time that it was impossible to observe "absolute neutrality and impartiality," even a decade after Bryce had applied to us the phrase. But in 1919 the tradition of the past was stronger than the pull of the future, and we slid back into our separated world and said emphatically that Europe was not our responsibility, the world was not our world. We still believed that we lived in the space of the Western Hemisphere, in the time of the nineteenth century. Space and time were disappearing as imperative categories in the physical world, but we were not ready in this other institutional world to abandon the comfort they had once vouchsafed us.

In the second war, so little time ago, isolationism was continually below the surface, ready to split the country when the fighting war was over, as it had split the country a quarter of a century before. Did Hiroshima end all isolationism? The atomic bomb was the final proof that the physical world was one. It seemed to follow that the political world must be one. Our manifest destiny—how nostalgic those irrevocable days of our youth—is no longer to grow from the shelter of our own roots and the strength of our own resources. In the long run isolation cannot continue. The people know that, even if they cannot foresee the implications. They are not happy in the knowledge. It is not easy to break with youth, to face the responsibilities of maturity. Even our political leaders cannot today find any consolation for the public in the habitual soothing dream world of a past generation. They must at last recognize—grudgingly or generously—that the United States is no longer divided from Europe; that separation, since it does not exist as a fact, cannot be a policy.

Historically it would be interesting to speculate on what causes—political, psychological, educational—had brought about our change in attitude since 1919. We had again, but on far vaster scale, poured out our money and had lost many more men than in the earlier war. The new relations that we were establishing were infinitely more "entangling" than in those earlier years. Our armies had landed on German and Japanese soil—and there they stayed. But "history does not exactly repeat itself."[11] The reasons for the apparent abandonment of our traditional policy of keeping out of Europe were doubtless complex and varied. We had come to know, to our grief, that to sell goods we must take goods in return; that it did not pay, in the long run, to lend money to those who wished to buy the fruits of our production if, at the same time, we excluded their products; that our high tariff barriers did not tend to increase the interflow of goods across the ocean; that, in fact, our competitors would retaliate by tariffs and preferences of their own; that foreign trade did count—the extra 8 or 10 per cent, the margin without which it was constantly harder to secure the stimulus to profit believed necessary for our expansion. The domestic market was no longer large enough.

But equally if not more significant was the change in political leadership in the field of foreign affairs. President Wilson's dream of a great league of all the nations in which we should play a leading role, tied to a just peace, had faltered and faded in the cynicism and national selfishness of his associates around the peace table in Paris and against the hostility and indifference of his fellow-countrymen at home. The people, immediately before the Paris Peace Conference, had repudiated the President's call in 1918 to save the world by electing a Democratic Congress. He refused to compromise, to accept suggested reservations, and stumped the country, gallantly yet obstinately fighting, on the edge of complete physical collapse, turning directly to the public. . . . The treaty was rejected. How far was the result due to the President's refusal to compromise and his disregard of the Senate, whose "advice and consent" were, after all, required by the Constitution when the President made treaties? No senator was taken to the Peace Conference or apparently consulted. Wilson insisted on making the ratification a personal and political issue. Yet in those years isolation was still deeply imbedded in American thinking. Was the time ripe? We are probably too near it for history yet to pronounce unqualified judgment, if indeed history, dealing so largely with the inarticulate minds of men, ever can.

In 1919 the implications of continuing our traditional policy of isolation, particularly after we had undertaken the responsibility of war and expanded our economy to meet its demands, were not so clear, and not yet experienced, as they were in 1946. Certain it is that the errors of American political disunity and withdrawal were not repeated. Long before the end of the war President Roosevelt began a practice not only of consulting with the Republican leadership in both House and Senate but of appointing their members to represent the nation in the negotiations that resulted in the United Nations and the other international agreements—a policy followed by President Truman. And the Republican leaders have co-operated in carrying out this informal undertaking—to keep American foreign policy out of partisan American politics and to coordinate executive and legislative in a joint program. At times there have been complaints on both sides that the other partner was not co-operating, but, on the whole, so far both parties have played the game, drawn together by attacks from the outside which Messrs. Molotov and Vishinsky impartially let fall on all alike, and the policy has worked. Senator Arthur Vandenberg, chairman of the Senate Foreign Relations Committee, has repeatedly urged this continuing nonpolitical cooperation. On November 3, 1947, he said: "Foreign policy is a legitimate subject of frank debate by our citizens. . . . It is a legitimate subject of partisan contest if there is deep division. But I raise the fervent prayer that we may ever strive for an unpartisan American foreign policy—not Republican, not Democratic, but American—which substantially unites our people at the water's edge in behalf of peace, with justice and liberty under law."[12]

Another difference between the worlds of 1919 and 1946 is worth remembering. The discovery and use of the atomic bomb by the United States altered the whole range and impact of war forever and the entire texture of peace. The secret of the bomb could not be kept by us—so our scientists who had invented it affirmed—and there was no defense against its use, they added. Even the axioms of war had gone, following the disappearance of the axioms of science. Hitherto the discovery of new engines of offense had been soon followed by the invention of new methods of defense—but now no longer. In a statement issued in the autumn of 1947 the Emergency Committee on Atomic Scientists[13] (Albert Einstein, chairman) declared that certain facts were accepted by all atomic scientists:

"1. Atomic bombs can now be made cheaply and in large numbers. They will become more destructive.

"2. There is no military defense against atomic bombs, and none is to be expected.

"3. Other nations can rediscover our secret processes by themselves.

"4. Preparedness against atomic war is futile and, if attempted, will ruin the structure of our social order."

Survival in the Air Age is the title of the report of the President's Air Policy Commission made on December 30, 1947. It is a study and recommendations not of a group of "brass hats" but of five distinguished laymen. These men are not alarmists. They do not agree with the scientists that "preparedness against atomic war is futile." But they are frank in stating the terrible scope of that preparedness. Let me quote from their report.

"Our national security must be redefined in relation to the facts of modern war. Our security includes . . . not having our cities destroyed and our population decimated in the process of our winning the first campaign. And it further includes not having our way of life, and particularly our civil liberties, taken from us in preparing for war. Our national security . . . can be assured only by the elimination of war itself. World peace and the security of the United States thus are now the same thing. . . . We will not be rid of war until the nations arrive at the great agreement to live together in peace. . . . There is almost no sign that this agreement will be made within the future with which the Commission has to deal. . . . Our policy of relative security will compel us to maintain a force in being in peace time greater than any self-governing people has ever kept."

In developing plans for our defense, the Commission assumes that "*possibly hostile powers will not be producing atomic weapons in substantial quantities before the end of 1952. . . .* Biological weapons are undoubtedly being studied in all parts of the world. . . . That extremely violent bacteria and viruses exist is common knowledge. . . . They can be distributed in our cities and among our crops and herds in advance, say a year or so, of a planned attack." Defense must be thought of in terms of offense. By the end of 1952 we must have, in addition to a strong defensive air equipment, "counteroffensive force built around a fleet of bombers, accompanying planes, and long-range missiles which will serve notice on any nation which may think of attacking us that, if it does, it will see its factories and cities destroyed and its war machine crushed."[14]

Thus we opened the Year of Grace 1948.

In a long generation wars had grown more universal, far more costly, involving finally the entire population. But hitherto this had meant years of slow preparation and organization—it was amazing that Germany could be ready in five years. Now a stroke of lightning—and the perfectly articulated military machine, with all its supporting paraphernalia of human beings, and tanks and guns, its raw and finished material, its tactics and strategy, would disappear into dust and gangrene. No secret, no defense. . . . Nuclear science, somewhat in advance of the art of political government, was one world, uncontrolled by two, or four, or fifty-seven operating in the choppy sea of balance of power.

That balance of power had shifted apparently overnight. In reality the slow disintegration of the British Empire and the gradual development of the British Commonwealth of Nations had been, since the first World War, preparing for an ultimate realignment and distribution of power, now suddenly becoming each day more apparent. For half a century the concentration of empire had been changing into the decentralization of federation, and, when the nations drew together to write their covenant, Canada, Australia and New Zealand, South Africa, and India, who had fought side by side with the mother-country, now in substance independent, came to the conference table as sovereign nations with the other nations. In these two brief years of 1946–47, India, Burma, and Palestine broke away, Southern Rhodesia was closer to dominion status, Egypt and the Sudan might follow, empire had given way to federation, an international pattern of what might occur on a larger scale. "Sir Hubert Rance, last British Governor in

Burma," runs a Reuters dispatch in the *New York Times* for January 5, 1948, "sailed down-river from Rangoon in the Royal Naval Cruiser Birmingham early today, cheered by thousands of Burmese citizens who lined the wharfs and river banks to bid farewell to the last representative of British rule in Burma. . . . The Union Jack that had fluttered from the mast of the Constituent Assembly Building was now stowed on board the Birmingham, on its way to Britain, where it will be kept in the British Museum." The old British Empire was gone.

The change is having and will continue to have far-reaching influence on American foreign policy. No longer over the world can we count on British power to balance and stabilize and control the restless ambitions of her lesser rivals for places in the sun, a power which in its exercise had been increasingly more friendly to American interests. President Monroe in his annual message of December 2, 1823, declared the famous doctrine—that the United States would, with force if necessary, resist any European attempted expansion in the Western Hemisphere—apparently only after the assurance of Canning, the British Foreign Secretary, that the British navy would support the United States.[15] During the next three and a half generations the United States expanded in the Pacific— Hawaii, Guam, the Philippines—taking on commitments not balanced by commensurate American seapower, even after our destruction of the Spanish fleet. We had placidly assumed that the Monroe Doctrine was a definition of our insulation from Europe, a detachment which most Americans imagined resulted solely from the good fortune of our position across the seas, an Act of God to his Chosen People. Had not President Monroe coupled his warning to foreign powers with the pronouncement that "in the wars of the European powers in matters relating to themselves we have never taken any part, nor does it comport with our policy so to do"?[16]

For these last two wars England had relied on our navy to see her through. After World War II American sea power was far greater than the combined navies of all other nations. We have grown out of the shelter of England's friendly arms. We must now look after our widely scattered commitments from Alaska to Manchuria with our own resources. The remark of Theodore Roosevelt, three years before the first World War, seems to have been realized: "In fact we ourselves are becoming, owing to our strength and geographical situation, more and more the balance of power of the whole globe."[17]

The gradual change in the form and essential structure of the British Empire into a federation of states was suddenly accelerated, soon after the war ended, into what looked more like a collapse of that empire, particularly in the East. Doubtless the freedom of India and the other members of the "confederacy" would have come irrespective of the strength of Britain. But the break would have been probably more gradual, over the course of evolving time, not with the sudden wrench of the now apparent fact that Britain was no longer able to hold them. She simply could not afford to sustain the life-lines of the old empire, to pay for her battleships, for her armies at the end of those lines, for the interest on her swollen external debt, for the social services to her own people which she had undertaken and was advancing. Her gold reserves were dangerously low, her securities largely liquidated to pay for the war effort, the balance of trade running against her, almost nothing left of the "service" of shipping and exchange that had helped to pay for imports in the old days. It was not now a problem whether she could meet the empire bill. Could she sustain her own tight yet delicate industrial economy and feed her people, or would she have to turn back to a green island of agriculture and support half her present population, the other half migrating to the shores of her lustier children, because she could not feed them any longer from the trade around the world that had made her the once mighty figure in the center? Bertrand Russell, if I remember rightly, had once made some such prophecy between the two world wars. Churchill may stab at the Labour government for giving away the splendid trophies of that empire world. It was the logic of events that was responsible for the yielding of these trophies.

We but now begin to realize the consequences of the disappearance of Britain from her ancient role as the political and economic center of the world. We see it in sudden withdrawals calling for immediate decisions on our part. She could no longer afford the cost of her share of German occupation; at her own request the job fell more and more to us. She pulled out of Greece; then we must slip into her place if the vacuum is not to be filled by another. She withdrew from Palestine; should we have taken over her responsibility for policing that troubled land, since the Security Council was not ready to act? Admission of Jews to Palestine was a policy popular in the United States, publicly advocated by the President. Yet, when partition was determined by the United Nations, we were unready to play our part to enforce it and allowed subsequent events to shape our course. Foreign policies, as Walter Lippmann has well said, should not be formed, and certainly not announced, until commitments and power have been brought into balance.[18]

Not only is Britain no more the center of world economy but that economy which she served and guided no longer exists. It had been built in the nineteenth century on principles of free trade. First among nations to industrialize, England accumulated vast surpluses which poured into the other countries to develop their potentialities. For well over the turn of the twentieth century the vast economic system, which England had begun, for which she acted as an international banker, ran smoothly on free trade and its necessary concomitant, free exchanges. England had but one basic raw material, coal, and depended on the sale of her manufactured goods and services to pay for the imports of raw material and food. She was not like the United States, the "new leviathan," whose industrial growth she helped to build—the United States, with her "vast internal market uncomplicated by tariff barriers, a social tradition entirely free of feudalism, a political system which put its emphasis on free organization, economic resources sufficient to fulfil any program of expansion, endless variety of climate, endless undeveloped land."[19] After the first World War it should have been apparent that the free economy of the nineteenth century, overlapping the twentieth, had disappeared in the economy of the new era, dominated by preferences, controls, and tariffs and no longer subject to the political, military, and financial influence of England. Nothing that the British government has done or any British government could do will change this fact.

The plight of Britain was not realized by our government in time to plan or chart the course we were bound to follow. It did not dawn on us in its full significance until the early spring of 1947, and its immediate effect was not then realized any more than its long-reaching repercussions are now understood. Vaguely there was talk, when the war ended, of two great nations now, the U.S. and the U.S.S.R., and of Britain not being in that class. But such talk missed sharpness of the point. It was not only that the might and hence the influence of Britain had shrunk; it was also that there was no other nation prepared to take her place and fill her role. The policy of the Kremlin was not to balance power but to absorb it. No other nation in Europe was strong enough to stem the spread of the "Holy Russian Empire." The United States had the strength. Did she have the courage, the experience, the desire, and, above all, the will to take the place of the United Kingdom?

In the life of the nations a vacuum has opened—the vacuum made by the withdrawal of Great Britain from the spaces of her influence. There are but two powers which can fill that vacuum, the U.S.S.R. and the U.S. The prophecy of De Toqueville, expressed over a hundred years ago, seems to have come true: "There are at the present time two great nations in the world . . . the Russians and the Americans. Both of them have grown up unnoticed; and while the attention of mankind was directed elsewhere, they have suddenly placed themselves in the front rank among the nations, and the world learned their existence and their greatness at almost the same time. All other nations seem to have nearly reached their natural limits . . . but these are still in the act of growth . . . along a path to which no limit can be perceived. . . . The conquests of the American are . . . gained by the plowshare; those of the Russian by the sword. The Anglo-American relies upon personal interest to accomplish his ends and gives free scope to the unguided strength and common sense of the people; the Russian centers all the authority of society in a single arm. The principal instrument of the former is freedom; of the latter, servitude. Their starting-point is different and their courses are not the same; *yet each of them seems marked out by the will of Heaven to sway the destinies of half the globe.*"[20]

II

NEW WORLD POLICY

✻

WHEN the history of these eventful years—1945–48—is written, what will perhaps be least understood is the attitude of the U.S.S.R.—at least until some future former commissar, if there is then a world in which it can be told, publishes his recollections of what went on behind the curtain. Russia historically has been likely to be troublesome in relation to her allies after a victorious war. Fed on victory, the great bear rises from her wounds and looks about for new fields to conquer. Her vitality is as unbounded as it is usually ill directed. Harold Nicolson has warned us against drawing too pat an analogy between the problems which now confront Europe and those which, following the climax of Waterloo, were settled in the Treaty of Vienna by Castlereagh, Metternich, and Talleyrand for nearly a hundred years of peace.[1] Napoleon's arms, as he invaded and conquered western Europe and made it a part of his empire, had terrified the world and consolidated England and Russia against him. Hitler, in the same manner as his ambitious predecessor, had revitalized and armed his weak and distracted country and conquered and incorporated most of Europe, all in less than a decade. And each had stubbed his imperial toe on Russian soil and had finally fallen after a Russian campaign. On each occasion Russia had helped to defeat the tyrant and, out of her victory, had emerged so powerful and so voracious as immediately to constitute the new threat to the dislocated European balance.

When the first World War broke out, Colonel House advised

President Wilson that "if the Allies win, it means largely the domination of Russia on the Continent of Europe"[2]—a consideration which had moved Theodore Roosevelt ten years before, at the outset of the Russo-Japanese War, to notify France and Germany that, if they supported Russia, he would "promptly side with Japan and proceed to whatever length was necessary on her behalf."[3]

But after the second World War the U.S.S.R. did not have the bomb, at least in any functional sense, and we did. Could she be certain that it might not drop on her during the time she was perfecting hers? Could she be absolutely certain that we would not fight, no matter how nasty and sustained the vilification, while she developed her own bomb at leisure? Was she making the same mistake that the German mind had once made—the conviction that American manhood was too soft, her government too timorously aware of the indifferent, pacific, unthinking American god, Public Opinion, to enter a war which must seem so distant from her shores? The bomb is close to every shore. Why, then, have the Russians resisted each plan for international atomic control? Even if, in a comparatively short time, she might perfect her own instruments of atomic world destruction, ours remained, and competition would be a touchy business, hardly calculated to produce the long peace which she so needed for the fruition of her domestic plans. Surely she could have tried some international co-operation, in spite of her fear of the capitalists, or played up that dread chiefly for domestic consumption behind the curtain. She did not trust us; but neither did we trust her, and yet we were ready to work with her to prevent this ultimate calamity.

One can but guess at the ambitions, the motives, the doctrinaire assumptions that guide the actions of the handful of these strange men who are controlling the destinies of their obedient and uninformed people. I saw their outlook operating in the tiny microcosm of the four nations which were trying the German war criminals at Nuremberg. The vitality of the Russians, their friendliness, their joy in drinking, dancing, singing, their pleasure in the direct contact of vigorous living; a certain shy dignity, like children at their first party; the sense of relative inferiority that youth has in the presence of years and experience; the fear that they might commit themselves in the forbidden path of political opinion; the repetition without discussion of sentimental clichés emptied of meaning ("our two great democracies" sort of thing); their endless oriental patience, watching to see if we could match them in disregard of time; their unalterable obstinacy once the "line" was taken, obviously from Moscow; that sense of a veil dropped over the unexpressed suspicion, more baffling because it is so often not unfriendly when there is no need for public unfriendliness—all these things make them not easy to understand.

I remember sitting next to one of Mr. Vishinsky's military aides at dinner when that gentleman had come to see the trial. We discussed poetry, music. He spoke of Mark Twain; I, of "The Twelve." We exchanged international amenities. "But let us be specific," I suggested. "I have always felt that our two nations could better understand each other if we were franker in stating what we really want." I swallowed another glass of vodka. "For instance," I continued, "the U.S.S.R., of course, has certain natural ambitions. What, for instance, do you want in the Dardanelles? Would you be content with a modified international agreement, and in what form?" He looked startled, straightened quickly.

"I am not permitted to discuss such matters of politics," he replied and paused. Then he concluded with the inevitable: "But I am certain that our two great democracies, etc." We both drank another vodka, and he touched my glass as if to imply that he had forgotten the indiscretion of my question.

I venture to think that we Americans tend to exaggerate the ingenuity and realism of Soviet politics, often forgetting how simple they are, and could understand them better if we remembered the uncritical acceptance of certain Marxian doctrines combined with great flexibility in the use of means, at any particular time, to accomplish the ends. Our admiration of Russian "realism" is like assuming that men, because they are silent, must also be strong.

Power the Soviets prize—and conquest. These are not qualities uncharacteristic of the human race. The Russians have accepted the doctrine that capitalism has the seeds of its own destruction within itself; that monopolies breed unemployment; and that unemployment and the suffering of the masses yield to the inevitable turn to communism, perhaps peaceful, sometimes bloody. They have seen the panic and depression that began in 1929; they look forward to its repetition, on a far greater and hence decisive scale in a year or two. Why should they try to prevent the inevitable if it drops the world into their lap? A policy of chaos seems to them not only logical but highly advantageous.

We had fought, or so most of us assumed, two wars to make the world "safe for democracy," yet in large areas democracy was fast disappearing. The laws and institutions on which we believed it to be built were being swept aside; the robot tramp of autocracy had but moved from a conquered country to one which was now a victor; the walls of political power which had held Soviet imperialism dammed had crumbled, and it had flowed across the Balkans, and immersed them, was lapping at the foundations of Greece, spattering France and Italy, perhaps tomorrow lashing back at Turkey and the Dardanelles. Had we to act to stem this flood? How could we feed the whole hungry world, and what, after all, would feeding do; feeding the Italians, for instance, from whom we were claiming no indemnity, to whom we had turned over our share of the captured battleships, whose close descendants peopled so much of our country, and to whom we had shipped vast quantities of relief since the war? These were the same Italians who apparently were turning more and more to Togliatti, who was organizing them into armed Communist brigades against the "Day." Yet what was the alternative? In November, 1947, the Communist riots began in Italy, and we were told that there were more men in the Italian Communist shock troops than were allowed Italy by the Allies under the treaty for her national army! . . . Four months later Czechoslovakia was absorbed.

We saw that communism—Communist imperialism—was fast spreading over all of Europe and in the Near and Far East. The Harriman Committee reported: "If the countries of middle-western and Mediterranean Europe sink under the burden of despair and become Communist, Scandinavia will fall into the same camp. The strategically and economically vital North African and middle-eastern areas will follow. This transfer of Western Europe, the second greatest industrial area in the world, and of the essential regions which must inevitably follow such a lead, would radically change the American position . . . [to] swift and complete conversion to a military footing which national security would require . . . the immediate and sweeping limitation of our economic and political life, perhaps extending even to our very form of government."[4] Control of the continents of Europe and of Asia would mean an industrial base for Soviet armed strength with greater resources than our own. Even if the desperate issue of war was beyond the realm of immediate calculation, an armed, united, and Soviet-dominated Eurasia would mean an armed United States, swiftly increasing in centralized power, under the daily (literally, since the atomic bomb) fear of war, as the ancient powers of Europe had always lived but from which, since our very beginning, we had been free. Did it follow that our country would be bathed in a climate of blatant and chauvinistic nationalism, the beginnings of which might be now seen rising here and there, in the "loyalty" tests, in the investigation of how men think and write in the moving-picture industry (in a congressional investigation the accused can have a lawyer, but the lawyer must not ask questions); a low growling hatred bred from fear, intolerance bred from fear, police methods bred from fear. "A state of near-hysteria now threatens to inhibit the freedom of genuine democrats," wrote the President's Committee on Civil Rights, in October, 1947, speaking through its chairman, Charles E. Wilson, president of the General Electric Company.[5]

We Americans, we free Americans, did not sound like our ancestors, about whom Walt Whitman had once said: "We have the air of persons who never knew how it felt to stand in the presence of superiors." No longer apparently could we live our lives so that we could look every damn man in the eye and tell him to go to hell! . . .

Such was the inexorable beat of history in these three eventful years. Yet, now that war was mainly over, Nature was pleased to take a cumulative hand in complicating, by her own simple devices, the desperate problems of the peace. There were added the terrible winter and the spring floods in England and drought all over Europe. In France the bread ration was cut because there had been, that summer, the worst harvest since the time of Napoleon. Increased famine and suffering made men despair of any quietly decent life, any moderate political solution. Europe turned to us for help, and the greatest responsibility that this nation has ever faced—perhaps, indeed, any nation—was laid before us by the swift march of stubborn events in a moment, while we were still rubbing our eyes, unable to believe what we saw rising to confront us in the comparatively placid life of our well-fed routine; understanding but dimly the savage realities, which might not come alive in the cold parade of figures, but which now and then troubled us when they spoke out of the eyes of pot-bellied children looking down from the moving-picture screen or in the faces of the gray-haired women marching in Paris in the ranks with workmen—Communists?—to protest against the increase in the price of bread, and we thought of Mme Defarge and the tumbrels.

The future student of these years of grace will seek origins and causes of the apparently sudden development of a United States foreign policy far broader and far different from anything we had ever conceived before. He will be interested in finding in the *Bulletin* of the State Department of October, 1944, the following statement: "If, by our providing help at this critical period, Italy can achieve economic and political conditions favorable to the development of democratic institutions and policies . . . our investment may be worth while."[6] He will ponder the extent to which the seeds of the European Recovery Plan could be found in President Truman's special message to the Congress on March 12, 1947, asking for immediate aid to Greece. The State Department has not made it clear why the urgency of that aid was not realized until a couple of weeks before the speech. "The need of Greece for large-scale economic and financial assistance from the United States presented itself late in February 1947 when the British Government found that it was no longer able to continue past March 31 the assistance it had been extending to Greece."[7] Yet in October, 1946, the prime minister of Greece, Mr. Tsaldaris, had told Secretary of State Byrnes that Greece needed financial assistance and military equipment. The appropriate officer in charge of surplus property in Europe was requested by Mr. Byrnes to assist Greece in every way possible. The Export-Import Bank could do nothing under the existing laws. The Porter Commission was sent to Greece in January, 1947, to make an economic survey. In December Mr. Bevin had indicated to Byrnes that England wanted to withdraw troops from Greece "and several other places" when it could be properly done; that she would continue to help with military equipment but "hoped" that we would provide economic assistance. Mr. Bevin did not say that the British troops would be withdrawn in March.[8] Moreover, Congress was asked to do far more than merely fill the gap caused by the British withdrawal. The seriousness of the approaching local crisis apparently had been realized, as so often occurs in a world of crises, when it was overripe. The British were slow to admit even to themselves that they no longer had the power to sustain their widely spread commitments.

Greece was immediately threatened by Communist domination. "I believe," said Mr. Truman, "that it must be the policy of the United States to support free peoples who are resisting attempted subjugation by armed minorities or by outside pressures." The two "ways of life" were sharply contrasted— "free institutions, representative government, free elections, guaranties of individual liberty, freedom of speech and religion, and freedom from political oppression" as against "the will of a minority forcibly imposed upon the majority . . . terror and oppression, a controlled press and radio, fixed elections, and the suppression of personal freedoms." It was made very clear that technical military assistance and supplies were to be furnished.

Was this to be a permanent policy of the United States? Was it to be enforced whenever we considered that "free peoples" were threatened? The Greeks were doubtless resisting "attempted subjugation," but were they a "free people" with the "free institutions" which the President described? How did such a policy fit with our obligations under the United Nations, assuming that they were not in a position to act?

If the question were referred to U.N., and the U.S.S.R. vetoed action, were we to act unilaterally? Did action extend to our sending troops into Greece to take the place of the British troops about to be withdrawn? Presumably, steps would be taken only after the request of the government in question, although that was not made clear.

The Greek-Turkish Aid Bill was signed May 22.

Western European reaction to the "Truman Doctrine" was troubled, suspicious, uncertain. Did this mean an imperial United States policy—armed intervention in the Mediterranean?

There was little language in the President's message to which the outlines of a broad European recovery plan could be traced. But the alarming unbalance of foreign trade was a pressing consideration which suggested that something must be done promptly. We had to have a new policy. On May 8, less than two months after the message, Undersecretary of State Acheson, in a speech at Cleveland, Mississippi, pointed out that our foreign exports of goods and services in the current year were estimated at sixteen billion dollars, an all-time peace high, against imports of eight billion. "Of this year's difference between imports and exports, more than five billion dollars is being financed by loans and grants-in-aid from the United States Government," the remainder of the enormous deficit by "private investments, remittances of American citizens abroad, and by drawing down the extremely limited foreign reserves of gold and foreign exchange." We had been lending money to help pay for our exports. The history which led to the depression of 1929 was repeating itself.

To what extent this speech was calculated to counterbalance any unfortunate "misunderstandings" of the Truman Doctrine, whether it was intended to suggest the outline of a new program in the nature of a "trial balloon," will be tempting subjects of speculation for our future historian. At least the speech was an official statement apparently announcing a radical and far-reaching foreign policy. It was not given as much publicity in the United States as might have been expected. The London *Times*, which printed the speech in full, commented editorially: "America must underpin the old world to maintain the balance of the new." To European observers it had tremendous significance. Was it the official American policy?

Mr. Acheson outlined three imperatives for our foreign policy: first, we "must take as large a volume of imports as possible from abroad" in order to narrow "the financial gap between what the world needs and what it can pay"; second, "the United States is going to have to undertake further emergency financing of foreign purchases if foreign countries are to continue to buy in 1948 and 1949 the commodities which they need to sustain life and at the same time rebuild their economies"; and, third, "we are going to have to concentrate our emergency assistance in areas where it will be most effective in building world political and economic stability, in promoting human freedom and democratic institutions, in fostering liberal trading policies, and in strengthening the authority of the United Nations."

Finally, the European Recovery Plan, the "Marshall Plan," as it was called for some time, was launched by Secretary Marshall in his historic announcement at Harvard on June 5. "The truth of the matter is that Europe's requirements for the next three or four years of foreign food and other essential products—principally from America—are so much greater than her present ability to pay that she must have substantial additional help or face economic, social, and political deterioration of a very grave character. . . . It is logical that the United States should do whatever it is able to do to assist in the return of normal economic health in the world, without which there can be no political stability and no assured peace.

Our policy is directed not against any country or doctrine but against hunger, poverty, desperation and chaos. Its purpose should be the revival of a working economy in the world so as to permit the emergence of political and social conditions in which free institutions can exist."

The President's message to the Congress had been a dramatic appeal against a tense background of nervous excitement. The Secretary spoke with cool deliberation, almost casually. The changed outlook was from piecemeal help from year to year to a co-ordinated over-all project to stimulate western Europe to reorganize its entire economy with our assistance, to build up its capital needs, to break down its intramural restrictions on trade, to open the routes of communication. Europe was to be put back in a position where it could produce and exchange goods once again.

That was the economic angle. The political approach was less clear. Mr. Acheson's third imperative, that emergency aid would have to be concentrated where it would be "most effective in building political and economic stability and in promoting democratic institutions," was not emphasized. Was it accurate to say that the policy was not directed against any doctrine? Was it to prevent the spread of communism or to rebuild the crumbling structure of the "free" governments? Was this one and the same thing, or was there a difference? For instance, if a nation without "assistance" from the Soviets freely chose communism as a way of government, or if a Communist party became dominant within her government, would she be excluded from the plan? If a satellite knocked at the door for help, was she to be admitted? Could Russia apply? Secretary Marshall's announcement apparently kept open that possibility. Yet there lurked a contradiction within its basic assumptions. For the plan certainly seemed to be limited to, or at least directed toward, countries that sustained certain liberties which we considered essential to democracies—and it was democracies that we were helping. This was a feature other than the economic and political approach, a moral and positive consideration. It sprang from the same impulse that lay behind our entry into both great European wars, a determination to help countries invaded by the totalitarian onslaught, in the belief that our own way of life was threatened by that onslaught. Russia's cold war was like Germany's—we dared not keep out.

Foreign policy does not achieve life as an expression of balanced and consistent formulas but takes shape under the pressure of conflicting considerations. Thus our approach to the problems of Europe had changed in emphasis between March 12 and May 8, and again on June 5, and will doubtless be further modified under the impact of actions over which we have no control. The Truman Doctrine stressed political considerations—help to Greece and Turkey to preserve their national independence free of Soviet domination. Secretary Marshall centered his exposition on economic inducements—"revival of a working economy"—which were not, however, disassociated from political ends—"the emergence of political and social conditions in which free institutions can exist."

Yet there is an apparent inconsistency between the doctrine and the plan. If the doctrine means that we are to help the nations whose institutions are democratic, to throw our lot in with them, to take our place as leading the free nations of the world, encouraging others to stand by their principles, how can we justify sending not only economic aid but arms to Greece, with its medieval and reactionary government?

To answer the question, we must define more clearly the differences which separate us from Russia. The fundamental issue is not ideological. The issue is Russian imperialism, an issue and contest of power. Aid to Greece is an effort to prevent that country from falling under the domination of Soviet dictatorship. It is an application of the principle of balance of power, as is the attempt to unite Europe politically. To Americans the doctrine of balance of power has often seemed "alien and unclean," a method by which the great powers manipulated and increased national antagonisms to further their own ends. That its application has been abused there can be no question. But it served successfully to keep the peace between 1815 and 1914. The precarious peace of today is threatened by the absence of any power on the continent of Europe to balance Russian aggression. As DeWitt C. Poole has pointed out: "The issue between the U. S. and Russia today is not private enterprise vs. Communism. The decisive issue is that between freedom and empire; between the idea of power centralized and uncontrolled as against power distributed and balanced."[9]

We may think of the phrase as un-American; the idea is not. It forms the basis of our constitutional organization, the balance of powers allotted among the various branches of government and between the federal and state systems. It has been recognized in the United States as a desirable foreign policy when the threat of world domination by a single nation arose. In 1911 Theodore Roosevelt, then on the editorial staff of the *Outlook*, said to a German diplomat: "As long as England succeeds in keeping up the balance of power in Europe, not only on principle, but in reality, well and good; should she, however, for some reason or other fail in doing so, the United States would be obliged to step in at least temporarily, in order to reestablish the balance of power in Europe, never mind against which country or group of countries our efforts may have to be directed." Four years later Woodrow Wilson told his friend, William E. Dodd: "I am as much a devotee of peace as any man; but in case Europe falls under the domination of a single militarist group, peace and democracy for our country are going to be in grave danger. In case that seems obvious, I shall have to urge American intervention"—which is precisely what the United States did in 1917. Thirty years later, by methods short of war, the same policy is being pursued.[10]

Only in those terms can the Greek and Turkish commitments be understood; and in those terms they are not inconsistent and can be justified. If Russia had not been in the picture, the considerations would obviously have been different. But to say that we are in Greece to support a reactionary government draws a false picture. We are in Greece in order to support *the existing government* and to help prevent it from falling under the domination of a militant Russia. We are in Greece to keep Russia out.

Such a policy has been called and will be called "power politics," a phrase even more distasteful to the average American ear than "balance of power." Both carry the implication of imperialism and an instinctive reaction against having any traffic with what from our experience of isolated immunity we think of as sordid European politics. But we must not let the compelling habit of a phrase hide the realities behind it or obscure the choice. Power politics is the only method, short of war, of creating or adjusting a balance of power; and we have fought two wars in order to balance power in Europe where we considered that unbalance threatened our own national interests. Making the choice is a responsibility which flows from our new position in the world today. That position involves the use of national power, which is, in essence, but a definition of diplomacy. The use of power always carries the risk of its misuse for the ends of imperialism. But it may also be employed to keep the peace of the world.

Nor was, as has been suggested, the Truman Doctrine abandoned or "absorbed" in the Marshall Plan. The essence of the former was the support given to going governments to resist subjugation; of the latter, help in rebuilding the economy of Europe. The policies are closely interrelated. The Soviet-directed insurrections and riots in Italy and France tended to solidify and broaden the doctrine, which, when announced, might have been tentative and limited. That there was no withdrawal or modification of the American position announced in the President's message was evident in his statement when the last American troops were withdrawn from Italy, on December 14, 1947, under the terms of the treaty, in language almost identical with that in the message. There was strikingly little criticism either on Capitol Hill or in the press of the President's warning to the Italian Communists. It was even said that he had not gone far enough. The Truman Doctrine had been extended to Italy. If her freedom is threatened, directly or indirectly, the United States "will be obliged to consider what measures would be appropriate for the maintenance of peace and security."[11]

Under the Monroe Doctrine we have resisted aggression against American nations in the Western Hemisphere; under the Truman Doctrine we may resist aggression against European nations in the Eastern Hemisphere.

The Truman Doctrine was originally, and the Marshall Plan has become, an expression of the policy of balance of power. Less than two months after the President had announced the doctrine, Premier Ramadier dropped the Communist ministers from the French cabinet. On June 1 Mr. de Gasperi followed suit in Italy. On November 10 the Secretary of State, testifying before the Joint Congressional Committees, made it clear that the U.S.S.R. was then excluded, saying: "Thus the geographic scope of our recovery program is limited to those nations which are free to act in accordance with their national traditions and their own estimates of their national interests." On December 19, in discussing E.R.P., he declared: "The success of such a program would necessarily mean the establishment of a balance in which the sixteen Western nations who have bound their hopes and efforts together would be rehabilitated, strong in forms of government which guarantee true freedom, opportunity to the individual and protection against the terror of government tyranny." Three months later five of these nations signed a cultural and political defensive treaty. The new American-European policy, whatever its origin, was now an acknowledged effort to block Soviet aggression.

But the Marshall Plan was originally announced as open to all nations. Bevin and Bidault met in Paris, apparently to consider how Mr. Molotov could be persuaded to join them as charter members—the European "big three." This was a minor diplomatic blunder, for, when he refused, Molotov could point his finger, with a little more appearance of justification, at the "conspiracy" against Russia when the time came for him to explain why he turned down an offer of help which all the countries in the satellite cluster so much needed. If Russia had come in, any consideration of helping only those countries whose political institutions were still free would, of course, have disappeared. Either the suggestion that *any* European country could join was hardly realistic when it was obvious that, in order to join, Poland, to take an example, would have to change her entire political and social structure from top to bottom; or the social and political aspects of the plan, that it was affording an economic base on which political freedom could take root, were meaningless. It is not, set in the terms of that dilemma, surprising that the U.S.S.R. did not appear enthusiastic about a scheme which invited her to join on the condition that she reform her political ways.

Mr. Molotov was doubtless peeved that the foreign ministers of England and France had talked things over in Paris before asking him to join them. But come he did, flanked by eighty-nine experts. That looked like business, and it may be assumed that he wanted the rest of the world to think that he was carefully studying the proposition. In a few days he left

in a huff and began to denounce the whole scheme as imperial-
istic. Yet, with any knowledge of American public opinion,
he could have counted on rejection by the Congress if he had
hailed the new approach, joined the other nations enthusiasti-
cally, and made great demands for help to the eastern bloc.
And what a play from the point of view of Russian propaganda: The United States of America votes down the last
chance for world unity and condemns Europe to a standard of
poverty! What a hole we would have been in if he had split
us by Russian friendship and co-operation, instead of uniting
us by opposition and vilification. It has been suggested that
joining in the plan for European recovery would have involved
the Soviet's opening their figures on production and foreign
trade and that they were unwilling to give these to the world.
That may be so; but their gesture of acceptance to our gesture
of inclusion would have meant little more than furnishing
such figures as they chose to submit.

Europe's response to the plan for European recovery was an
amazed and excited jubilance. Bevin "grabbed at it with both
hands!" Was this the same nation as the America of 1919?
Was our isolationism a thing of the past? What a revolution
in the relation of the United States to Europe! The State Department yielded to the change in the same manner that so
often the Supreme Court has found it necessary to alter the old
law to fit the new facts—by the use of "a fiction intended to
beautify what is disagreeable to the sufferers."[12] It tried to
bridge the past that was no longer to the future that might be
by asserting that the Marshall Plan was "in the direct line of
American policy from the earliest days of the Republic."[13]

Success of the Marshall Plan, in the minds of its sponsors, is
conditioned on the belief that trade between eastern and western Europe can be re-established. That trade exists today, and
it is thought that the economic pressure for goods to be ex-

changed along the routes they had followed for a thousand years—grain from the East and manufactured goods from the West—will be stronger than any political attempts to dam the natural flow. Bulgarian peasants who need farm implements will not refuse to receive them because they have been made by French workmen who do not happen to be Communists; and Socialists in Great Britain will not turn away from wheat grown by Communists in the Ukraine. If trade flows, perhaps the economy of Europe can be rebuilt. If it does not, no outside help can revitalize that economy. The weakness in "balancing" a united Europe against Russia is that western Europe is not and perhaps can never be a self-contained economic organism. On the other hand, it is doubtful whether Russia can supply the needs for manufactured goods of the satellite countries which constitute eastern Europe. It is a little hard to envisage an increased trade accompanying political withdrawal of the West from the East. It should have precisely the opposite effect. Yet will Russia permit a *rapprochement*? That is the dilemma with which we are faced.

Henry L. Stimson, twice Secretary of War, once Secretary of State, his faith and courage no less bright than when he had joined the army to fight for his convictions, said these words: "We Americans today face a challenging opportunity, perhaps the greatest ever offered to a single nation. It is nothing less than a chance to use our full strength for the peace and freedom of the world."[14]

Apparently we have made the choice—made it at least in general terms. And what a choice it is! The last bridge to our own dear American past is burned and gone. It is too early to know to what extent we will wrangle over our responsibility before we accept it as inevitable. Here on this continent a new democracy dedicated itself to the proposition that all men are created equal and three generations later fought a war made inevitable by the refusal of a great section of that democracy to accept the proposition. A benevolent Providence, we might think, had permitted us to practice our experiment in self-rule under ideal conditions of freedom and resources, hardly touched by the ancient inheritances of class privilege which inhibited the older world. We were given a handful of years to prove the reality of our dreams, to establish our power to sustain them, to create a philosophy of virtue that would make them actual. We were allowed to mature. And now suddenly, as we emerge in the full flush of our powers, more apparent against the wretchedness of all the rest of the world, we are asked to take responsibility for that poor world; to help and to lead; to stand with other freedom-loving countries to preserve their freedom; not to dictate to them how they should govern, not to impose our mass culture on their more qualitative and far more ancient civilizations, but to help them organize and pull together their crumbling economic systems. Is not the ability to organize the material world peculiarly a gift of the Americans? Can we do these things, suddenly become urgent against the alternative of two armed worlds, balancing a bomb between them? Can we do this—hold together for a time this human world, so that it will grow, as we had been growing, closer to realizing democracy? "We have frequently printed the word Democracy," Walt Whitman wrote, "yet I cannot too often repeat that it is a word the real gist of which still sleeps, quite unawaken'd, notwithstanding the resonance and the many angry tempests out of which its syllables have come, from pen or tongue. It is a great word, whose history, I suppose, remains unwritten, because that history has yet to be enacted."[15]

Perhaps the history of the word "democracy" is now to be written.

III

THE WORD "DEMOCRACY": INDIVIDUAL
LIBERTY AND EQUALITY

✼

THE content and direction of a new political movement cannot be appreciated if it is looked at from a single angle. History is not to be interpreted solely in economic terms. Nor is insight into its movement furnished by those who believe that we should look only to "human" causes, to the "psychological" phenomena which they claim to find below the surface of all economies. Nor has the last word been said by that school of thought which sees the rise and decline of nations in terms of biological life, drawing charts to indicate their conception of a universal movement. The movement of history cannot be oversimplified by definition or the application of a single theory. Because it fits no theory, it has the appearance of inconsistency. This to the average observer, in search of simplification, particularly if it be moral, is confusing and unsatisfactory. Yet the difficulty is not so much that the movement of life is inconsistent as that it is varied and complex. The human eagerness to find a single cause is continually being thwarted by the conflicting sources of human behavior. As a result, the policy of a nation and its diplomacy over any given period of years often seem, when we are still close to them, contradictory, timorous, or illogical. They hardly ever "make sense." The purpose and end of war is comparatively direct and easily understood. Its aim is clear—victory—even if the strategy may be confused or uncertain. Peace can never have "the moral equivalent of war," to use a phrase of William

James. When peace is restored, we soon again have the sense of indirection and confusion which war has temporarily banished.

To describe the plan for assistance to Europe as being limited to those countries which sustain democratic institutions, or aimed solely to permit their national survival, would not be accurate, any more than it could be adequately defined as an attempt at economic revival without reference to the political consequences. Western Germany is apparently to be admitted; and, if Spain is eventually added, it will be from considerations of interrelated economic interests, linking her with the West, and obviously not from a desire to support her institutions. Yet it cannot be said that the encouragement of democratic governments is not a major consideration. The truth is that the United States has several interests, moral and economic, yet also strategic and political, in helping the participating countries to achieve a balanced recovery.

If emphasis on democratic institutions and policies is an important element in the new program, we must find out what our conceptions of democracy mean not only to us but to Europeans. Their ideas of the democratic state may be more qualified than ours, or ampler, perhaps more precise. Assumptions by an American and by a European of what constitutes Western civilization may be superficially alike on the material surface of the twentieth century; their differences must be taken into account if there is to be integration of purpose in a common effort. Where will Europeans yield, what should we abandon, on what insist? What changes in our thinking, and in theirs, will be needed to define this new approach, so that it may be understood and accepted?

The heart of our American tradition is the integrity of the individual. This theme has been constantly affirmed and repeated throughout our history, cherished and sustained from one generation to another. It emphasizes the individual as against the state; the single human being in contrast to the mass, differentiation rather than uniformity. "Those who won our independence," wrote Mr. Justice Brandeis, "believed that the final end of the state was to make men free to develop their faculties. . . . They believed liberty to be the secret of happiness and courage to be the secret of liberty." He often repeated this proposition in words that cannot be forgotten. "America, dedicated to liberty and the brotherhood of man, rejected heretofore the arrogant claim that one European race is superior to another. America has believed that each race had something of peculiar value which it could contribute to the attainment of those high ideals for which it is striving. America has believed that in differentiation, not in uniformity, lies the path of progress. Acting on this belief, it has advanced human happiness and it has prospered."[1]

Recently this American faith was eloquently expressed by David E. Lilienthal, as he interrupted a barrage of questions by Senator Kenneth D. McKellar at a hearing of the Joint Congressional Committee on Atomic Energy, which was considering the confirmation of the former T.V.A. head as chairman of the new Atomic Energy Commission. "I believe," Mr. Lilienthal said, "and I do so conceive the Constitution of the United States to rest upon, as does religion, the fundamental proposition of the integrity of the individual; and that all Government and all private institutions must be designed to promote and to protect and defend the integrity and the dignity of the individual; that that is the essential meaning of the Constitution and the Bill of Rights, as it is essentially the meaning of religion."[2]

I do not mean to suggest that this ideal is an American invention or that we have realized its implications. Of course we have not. The idea springs from Christian morality, common to all peoples of Christendom. It has been the solace of the poor and oppressed throughout the Dark Ages, the medieval world, and the Renaissance. It is rooted in a profound faith in human personality. But, since the skepticism and pragmatism of the modern scientific age seized men's minds, the emphasis has shifted from the future to the present, and men have come to believe and to insist that their well-being might be achieved here and now as well as in some future state of being. They are no longer satisfied with the once infinite comfort of an untroubled faith in a future heaven. In the tumultuous rush of the modern world—Galileo, Newton, Darwin, steam, electricity, Einstein—the masses discovered the present and insisted on sharing at least a part of it. The conception of individual integrity and equality from birth to death, irrespective of inequalities which might thereafter be apportioned, with an eye on the immediate and the material, as contrasted with the hereafter and the spiritual, is, relatively speaking, recent.

It is a conception which the Western world rather than the East has accepted. Where hopeless and changeless poverty exists, the imagination of a starved body will dwell in dreams that can be gratified only after life is done. Acceptance of an ordained environment, a sense of fatalism, of futility, are likely to spring from an environment where death is the only relief from suffering. In our world today the Western conception of individualism—Christian, yet conscious and pragmatic—has only begun its expanding ferment in certain areas of the East and has left great masses of people unmoved by impulses which have been so fruitfully active in the West. In America this belief in the integrity and value of the individual human being has achieved general acceptance and has been more broadly translated into material action than in any other country which has inherited the western European culture.

I say "fruitfully active" because our faith in human individual worth lies at the basis of our success in improving his material lot. If he can change his environment, the future is not foreclosed by the past. "Of all the peoples of the world," wrote No Yong-Park, a Chinaman educated in a Buddhist monastery and at Evansville College and Northwestern and Harvard universities, "Americans, to my mind, are the most progressive. They are the ones who live in the future tense. . . . They do not care to know from where they came. . . . The Chinese notion of progress has been to struggle to catch up with their fathers, whereas the American idea is to do something which no one has yet done."[3]

But belief in the value of that material improvement is not, often to our surprise, everywhere shared. Our approach to life appears to the mystic and contemplative mind to be superficial, vulgar, and selfish. Such a mind cannot understand or approve the expression of our civilization in our art or the virtues of personal creativeness which to us constitute its glory and changing freshness. The mystic's life-current finds expression in the anonymous, the racial, the unchangeable. Competition, the practical application of our belief, seems to him calculated to bring about a world from which the beauty and value of life are disappearing, where the eternal values have been sacrificed to strident trivia. That wolf eat wolf, he suggests, is a precise description of a world discovered by Darwin, projected by Herbert Spencer, and perfected by the American businessman. But such a philosophy and practice, he adds, do not lead to the threshold of the only true world—the world of the spirit.

Let us for a moment, to contrast extremes, compare the methods of the late Mohandas K. Gandhi and John L. Lewis. Both were leaders of many men. Each used power over the multitude to achieve his ends, the one by spiritual, the other by material, pressure. Mr. Gandhi broke his fast of one hundred and twenty-one hours when he was convinced that it had achieved its purpose of improving harmony for the Indian Union. Yet, somehow, I cannot picture Mr. Lewis fasting one hundred and twenty-one hours to attain greater co-operation among the American Federation of Labor, the United Mine Workers of America, and the Congress of Industrial Organizations.

I have contrasted the East with the West. The differences, it may be said, are not typical of those which separate European from American thought. But they are not dissimilar. The European of today, though greatly admiring American material achievements, often questions the standards of American civilization and is skeptical of its moral results. The immense emphasis on individual values seems to him too often channeled into mere business competition, where the integrity of the individual is soon forgotten. He points to the continually increasing contraction of power and wealth as an inevitable result of individualism run wild. Indeed, he concludes, the differentiation of which Justice Brandeis and Mr. Lilienthal speak is disappearing in America and may be found far more in European countries, where the past is still a part of the lives of men, and the slower and closer life of the community, with its greater sense of reverence and ritual, frees the spirit in ways that cannot be achieved by the doctrine of free moral and economic enterprise.

Hugo Munsterberg, a German, after teaching psychology for a dozen years at Harvard, was impressed, in analyzing the American character in his book *The Americans*, by "the instinct for free self-initiative which has set in motion this tremendous economic fly-wheel. . . . The economic life means to the American a realizing of efforts which are in themselves precious. It is not the means to an end, but is its own end. . . . The European of the Continent esteems the industrial life as honest, but not as noble."[4]

Almost as cardinal as the importance of the individual is our belief in equality. Most Americans would, I think, assert that any true democracy was founded on that belief. And yet it is obvious that democrats in other nations do not share that assumption or agree on our conception of equality. Few would deny that England has evolved a system as essentially democratic as ours, and many believe that in England the diversity which Brandeis thought was America's aim—tolerance of eccentricity, if you like, to leave room for the rare quality of flavor—has been achieved more than with us in the United States, where, they would insist, a drab uniformity is the inevitable result of the American worship of equality.

The existing social and economic equality amazed the early observers of the American scene. Michel Guillaume de Crèvecoeur, in the third essay of his *Letters from an American Farmer*, written sometime in the late 1770's, said of America: "Europe contains hardly any other distinctions but lords and tenants; this fair country alone is settled by freeholders, the possessors of the soil they cultivate, members of the government they obey, and the framers of their own laws, by means of their representatives."[5] When immigrants extolled America as a land of equal opportunity, they meant not only that all men were equal before the law but that the New World was a place where anyone had a chance to become economically secure. The chance was not one afforded by any theory of government or result of revolution, except in so far as government put no impediment in the way of material success. It was the unchecked access to the land and its resources, which lay fallow and undeveloped.

The immense part that this belief that all men are (and should be) equal played in our manners and institutions is constantly the theme of De Tocqueville and of Bryce. That equality of condition had actually been largely attained in the young republic struck the former observer, who thought that the passion for equality was stronger than the desire for liberty, although the people had never been confronted by the "formidable alternative"—an alternative which has not been resolved, as we shall presently see, by the simple expediency of dispensing with liberty, on the assumption that a destruction of individual liberty was necessary before equality could be achieved, which only the state could provide.

The inconsistency between insistence on freedom of the individual and abandonment to the domination of the multitude impressed the logical and philosophic mind of the Frenchman more than Bryce's objective and balanced observation. De Tocqueville was torn between his great admiration for the new democratic experiment, with what seemed to him its inevitability, and his nostalgic and somewhat romantic admiration for the aristocratic tradition, with its "proud contempt of physical gratifications which is sometimes to be met with even in the most opulent and dissolute aristocracies" but never in the "wealthier inhabitants of the United States." He dreaded the leveling process which would tend to make men not the revolutionary individuals who would hate and resist despotic power but the docile wards of a benevolent state devoted to their material well-being. He saw in the changing world that was shaking off the old tyrannies "an innumerable multitude of men, all equal and alike, incessantly endeavoring to procure the petty and paltry pleasures with which they glut their lives . . . reduced to nothing better than a flock of timid and industrious animals, of which the government is the shepherd."6

Lord Bryce, content, in most instances, to let the facts speak for themselves, distrustful of explaining social phenomena in terms of political causes, not tempted to yield to the Frenchman's large moral generalities, nevertheless met him on common ground in recognizing the uniformity of American life. American cities, he found, were all alike; "their monotony haunts one like a nightmare"; there is less variety among men than in Europe; although life "may be pleasanter, easier, simpler," it is not capable of the intensity that may be found in a great European center. He was unwilling to ascribe the result to a democratic form of government. He pointed out that equality could exist as well in an autocratic as in a democratic state. The equality of material conditions explained much of the uniformity.[7]

I have quoted at perhaps undue length from De Tocqueville and Bryce, because they seem to me still to be the most sympathetic yet acute critics of the American scene. These reactions are in the main as significant today as when they were first set down. And they have been repeated by many subsequent observers. Edward Dicey, Matthew Arnold, Paul Bourget, Victor Vinde, covering a period of eighty years from 1863 to 1942, have all testified to the singular uniformity of American habits and thought.[8]

In its discussions of the "Ideal of Freedom and Equality" the President's Committee on Civil Rights states: "This concept of equality which is so vital a part of the American heritage knows no kinship with notions of human uniformity or regimentation. . . . In our land men are equal, but they are free to be different."[9] To this a European might observe that Americans are certainly permitted to be free but in fact are not so free as men in older countries, where the belief in equality has not grown into the belief that no one should be unequal and that a form of life that is good enough for most people is good enough for *all* people; that, though Americans have a *right* to think differently, in fact their thinking, like their industry, is that of the mass. And he might conclude by quoting from *Main Street* or from *Middletown*.

It is worth, I think, pursuing the discussion of equality a little further. As an American ideal, just how far does it reach? Is it essential to democracy, or is it ultimately antipathetic to liberty, as De Tocqueville seems to suggest? To what extent has the growth of the ideal of the service state affected the democratic doctrine of equality?

To Americans equality meant, above all, equality of political opportunity, the essential counterpart of individual liberty. Both were expressions of the revolt against the excesses of government, directed against its disregard of personal rights, insisting that *under the law* all men should be equal. The equality that the Revolution brought about was a political, not an economic, equality. No one would have then dreamed of advocating a system under which wealth should be more evenly distributed. Equality of opportunity meant that the law should treat all men alike and that social and political inequalities should not be created or perpetuated by law. The theory of the service state had not been suggested in a society in which such obviously public functions as the distribution of the mails and the cleaning of streets were still performed by private operation. Individual liberty did not and was not intended to establish anything more than political equality, and rights were conceived of as legal and political, not as economic or industrial.

In Europe the revolt against legal, social, and political privilege had "emancipated economic initiative from monopolies, from the decaying remnants of the gilds, and from obsolete systems of state control, and . . . set the new aristocracy of wealth on a footing of parity with the old aristocracy of land."[10] But state monopolies, guilds, the land-tenure system which in Europe chained the peasants to the land, and aristocratic inheritance did not exist in young America, where land was free and social stratification nonexistent. Class distinctions, on the whole, had not followed the earlier English settlers into the unknown land. The environment of the raw material of frontier life was hardly calculated to develop such distinctions. Primogeniture and, with the exception of one section of the country, large landholdings, the basis of any landed aristocracy, were not inherent to American institutions. At the time of the Civil War the small individually owned farms of the North and West were still typical of American agricultural society.

This was not true in the South, where the tradition of landed gentry, their power based on the immense plantations operated by slave labor, had for many generations been firmly established. This group had politically dominated the country almost from the beginning. The Civil War, the "Second American Revolution," as the Beards have called it, was a struggle between the planting aristocracy of the South and the farmers, businessmen, and artisans of the other sections of the country. "It was . . . a social war . . . making vast changes in the arrangement of classes, in the accumulation and distribution of wealth, in the course of industrial development."[11] The war broke the power of the only "class" which had grown out of the American experiment in the sense that "class" is used to designate a society where differences are sharply marked by "superiors" and "inferiors"; where land is held by a closely integrated minority and tilled by "inferiors" (serfs or slaves); and where the aristocratic tradition is based on an accepted recognition of those differences as part of the order of things. The doctrine of equality of opportunity achieved new vigor as the result of the conflict. Social equality was very real, and an equal chance in the economic field of free land and untapped resources was more actual than anywhere else in the world. There were no extremes of wealth and poverty. Americans were largely self-supporting, living from the land. Comparatively few were dependent on the uncertainty of a wage system. In a word, the problems of an industrial society did not exist.

As the politically free community of the eighteenth and the first half of the nineteenth centuries developed into the great modern industrial society of today, power and wealth became more and more concentrated in fewer hands. Economic equality largely disappeared. The economic inequality that followed under the "free" economy of the Manchester School was in sharp contrast to the political liberty, and less and less equality and liberty seemed two sides of a single ideal. The process was gradual. The class distinctions that had survived the Industrial Revolution in England, where an aristocracy of wealth had been substituted for an aristocracy of land, never took hold of the institutions of the younger country, a fact which tended to obscure the change. Those, however, who noted the rapidly increasing economic extremes, and the enormous growth of industrial concentration, were concerned that the wide chasm of class which had always been characteristic of English society might be approaching in America. They observed the aspects of certain of the modern giants, who at times owned and policed the towns in which their employees lived, armed and used private troops to break strikes, and influenced the press and educational institutions to further their business ends. These activities have aspects of sovereignty, just as international cartels by the use of penalties and preferences in pooled agreements levy tariffs on goods for import or export with the same results on prices as are achieved by the tariffs of governments.

It was not until these differences emerged from the maladjustments of the new industrial civilization that the philosophy of the service state slowly began to appear. Such conditions demanded more state direction, and we shall elsewhere note how this direction has increased in accordance with the growing needs of society. The benefits rendered by the state grew progressively, and the cost of those benefits were paid out of increased taxes on the surplus wealth which the system was producing. The state was in fact offering more than the equality of being treated alike under the law; it was giving to everyone roads and sewers, a cheap postal system, garbage disposal, parks, museums, playgrounds, libraries, electric lights, and free elementary education. It had begun to furnish, to some extent at least, equal services—municipal hospitals, milk for school children, slum clearance, and low-cost housing. This was a new conception of equality of opportunity, for it meant an equalization by the state of those opportunities without which it was believed individual ability and energy could not emerge. It was grounded on the growing conviction that only in some measure of economic equality can the variety of human life find full expression and that uniformity is developed and increased by the stratification of class which derives from the economic inequalities which an uncontrolled industrial system necessarily creates. There is increasingly a wide belief that a greater equality of economic environment is needed to give individuals a chance to achieve some freedom of the personality in the industrial organization of the present day. Such freedom breeds the energy of the spirit, which is the base of all vital culture. At best great inequalities of wealth create social classes where "a cloistered and secluded refinement, intolerant of the heat and dust of creative effort, is the note, not of civilization, but of the epochs which have despaired of it . . . and have sought compensation for defeat in writing cultured footnotes to the masterpieces they are incapable of producing."[12]

I do not suggest that equality of economic opportunity is intrinsic to the American ideal. It has, indeed, hardly reached articulate expression, let alone general acceptance. But I believe that it is the motive that underlies much of the social work of government in America at this time.

Expressing its "ideal of freedom and equality," the President's committee said: "We can tolerate no restrictions upon the individual which depend upon irrelevant factors such as his race, his color, his religion or the social position to which

he is born."[13] Is a slum an irrelevant factor—disease, poverty?
The modern state is broadening the field of equality.

A hundred years ago the world was witnessing the evolution in governments from monarchical and autocratic to democratic institutions, as a result of the impetus given by the
American and French revolutions. Today this tendency is re-
versed. Even before World War I the people had begun to distrust their political institutions. "Public confidence in them
has manifestly declined," A. Lawrence Lowell wrote in 1913,
"and with increasing rapidity of late, until it almost seems
that the American people are drifting toward a general loss of
faith in representative government."[14] In the years immediately preceding World War II there was much open criticism of
the structure and efficiency of republican institutions. The reaction was not back to the glittering traditions of monarchy
but to the more compulsive and more powerful tyranny of the
totalitarian state, with its promise of equality and security
shrouded in a medieval atavism, couched in the myths of
racism and of national glory, and armed with the modern instruments of mass control. It was equipped with the apparatus
of propaganda, exploitation of fear and hatred, the goose step
and the concentration camp. Russia, Italy, Germany, Spain,
and finally the Balkans embraced the order of the new tyranny.
Even in the countries which had not sacrificed their freedoms
there was, at least before the war, open criticism of democratic principles, and in places an almost triumphant admiration of the new saviors, who had brought good roads and
regular trains and discipline—Mussolini, Hitler, Franco—until the war showed us the virtue of our own free political institutions.

This revolt against democratic institutions springs, I venture to suggest, from a conviction held by great masses of
people that political liberties, which are the foundations of

the democratic state, have proved sterile and ineffective. What good is the vote—so runs the complaint—if we are out of work and our children go hungry? What have all these political paper advantages brought to our lives? Let us march on Rome; we cannot vote ourselves full bellies. What stirs men today in most sections of the world is no moving vision of political freedoms, particularly where they have never been largely felt and enjoyed, but the simple needs of shelter and of food, pressing daily. The Communists, knowing this, do not preach Marxian dialectics, except to the inner circle, but promise employment to the workers in Milan, land to the Breton peasants. The narrow choice between security and personal liberty is made to seem inescapable. And who will choose freedom if the state will give him bread? These are false interpretations, for, without the solid underpinning of political rights, liberty and soon equality are without support, and we have but marched back to slavery. But this is not to say that political freedom need be the only jewel in the democratic crown or that any doctrinaire notion of the form that economic freedom must take should prevent us from achieving a greater economic equality if that freedom is to be actual. Thus seen, equality is no longer an alternative to freedom but a condition for its fruition.

IV

THE WORD "DEMOCRACY": YOKE OF
THE MULTITUDE

✲

LORD ACTON has somewhere said that the most certain test by which to judge whether a country is really free is the amount of security enjoyed by minorities. The President's Committee on Civil Rights in its now famous report dealt, necessarily, largely with the rights of minorities, to what extent they were in practice supported under the law, how much infringed. Of the four classifications under which the committee grouped the results of its study, the third, "The Right to Freedom of Conscience and Expression," covered only a few pages, which discussed chiefly the loyalty tests for civil servants. The freedoms which comprise this right—religion, speech, press, and assembly—the committee thought were substantially secure and for this reason, and because an extensive study in the field was being made by others, did not investigate the extent of their protection. There can be little doubt, I think, that Americans are relatively free in these respects. The First Amendment has been jealously guarded by the Supreme Court, and laws do not, generally speaking, interfere with religious tolerance or with a free press. We are legally free to think and say what we like. This is a great achievement of which we are quite properly proud.

Yet because men have the right to speak freely does not necessarily mean that they will do so. Censorship and the impending threat of police interference prevent any free criticism, any honest climate of public opinion, from developing in countries where the press is not free. But there are subtler forces which tend to limit an open and vigorous exchange of thought, so essential in any unobstructed and dynamic society. Of these, one of the most compelling in the United States is the power of majority opinion and its tendency to exclude or discourage the expression of views which are opposed to that opinion. I have spoken of the emphasis which our American democratic society places on equal opportunity. I should like to consider, at this point, the relation of the doctrine of equality to the minority and the effect of majority public opinion on minority thinking.

The essence of a successful democratic government is that, when a political decision has been made by the majority, it cannot be questioned by the minority. The fundamental assumption is that public opinion, once it has been found sufficiently durable to be more than a passing whim, should be put into effect. This hypothesis is not based on any belief that the majority of the people are always right but that in the long run the people can better judge of their needs than any special group exercising a vicarious judgment, however benevolently, of what those needs are. Democrats also believe that the constant exercise of their political rights by the people not only achieves a happier and more united nation but develops the strength and wisdom of the individuals who exercise those rights. Yet, if the people are to bow to the opinion of the majority, it is necessary to be as certain as possible what that opinion is. "The devotee of Democracy is much in the same position as the Greeks with their Oracles. All agreed that the voice of an oracle was the voice of a god; but everybody allowed that when he spoke he was not as intelligible as might be desired."[1] The essential place of the minority in a democracy is to test, to challenge, to dispute the claim that any particular voice speaks for the majority until public opinion has had an opportunity of being informed on the relevant facts and of reaching a considered conclusion.

The men who drafted the Constitution saw that in order to prevent usurpation by the sovereign—the new government—power had to be vested in the people themselves. But they were by no means confident that the people would exercise this power wisely and with becoming restraint. Roger Sherman, of Connecticut, a delegate to the Constitutional Convention, insisted that the election of representatives to the House ought to be by the state legislature and that "the people immediately should have as little to do as may be about the Government. They want information and are constantly liable to be misled." Elbridge Gerry, from Massachusetts, agreed with him: "The evils we experience flow from the excess of democracy." Madison, although he was in favor of the popular election of one branch of the national legislature, was "an advocate for the policy of refining popular appointments by successive filtrations" and was opposed to direct election of the President or of senators. "Where a majority are united by a common sentiment, and have the opportunity," he contended, "the rights of the minority party become insecure."[2] So the delegates put a brake on the use by the people of their new and potent instrument by making the government representative and participation by the people indirect. The President was to be elected not by the people but by electors, who were in turn chosen by the people. Senators were made the choice of the state legislatures, not the direct choice of individual voters. "The six-year term of the Senators, expiring biennially by thirds, was meant to be a brake on the immediate will of the people." It was a body, as Madison said, "admirably organized to protect the minority of the opulent against the majority" and "to secure the permanent interests of the country against innovation."[3] The new government was

curbed and checked by a complicated series of balances and
distribution of activities. Correspondingly, the people, to
Hamilton "a great beast," had to be restrained by appropriate
arrangements for the exercise of a vicarious dominion.

There has been no change in the Constitution giving greater
power to the executive or to the legislature. The balances between them have remained as they were originally written.
The veto and the power to override it; the function of the
Supreme Court to declare void both state and federal laws
which the Court found to be unconstitutional, even by the
margin of a single vote; the separation of the three functions
of the national government; the territory in which national
and state governments respectively function—these ultimate
bulwarks against the abuse of sovereign authority have not
been modified by constitutional amendment.

But the limits on the expression of the popular will have
been radically altered. The electorate has been greatly increased
not only by action of the states, which have constantly tended
to enlarge the voting base by eliminating property and other
qualifications on the privilege of voting, but by amendments
to the national Constitution: the Fifteenth, admitting Negroes; and the Nineteenth, giving women the ballot. Under
the Seventeenth Amendment, senators are now directly chosen
by the voters. And, by one of those rare changes in the Constitution by usage rather than by formal amendment, the
presidential electors have in practice lost their right to exercise discretion in choosing the President, and the people actually elect him directly, although their vote is taken through
state units.

Thus, while the inhibitions imposed on the national government and its various branches have remained unchanged,
the direct participation of the electorate in the affairs of government has been greatly enlarged, and two of the original

constitutional limitations on the exercise of this power, making it indirect and representative, have been removed.

The tendency to turn toward more direct popular government, steadily increasing in more recent times, was evident in the introduction in a number of states of the initiative, referendum, and recall. Many matters of legislation were referred directly to the people, and decided by them, under provisions of their state constitutions requiring or permitting popular decision on specified matters—increase of state or municipal indebtedness, public operation of utilities, use of certain types of taxation such as the progressive tax on chain stores. The people were even asked to take direct part in administrative functions, to recall judges and other public servants if their work proved unsatisfactory. Theodore Roosevelt even went a step further, advocating extension of public participation in the function of the judiciary. On the day that he announced that his hat was in the ring for nomination by the Republicans to the presidency in 1912, he delivered an address advocating the recall of judicial decisions by the people.

As the "direct" participation of the people in their government, in theory at least, was constantly increasing, the range of those subjects with which the government dealt was growing even faster. No one could possibly be conversant any longer with all the activities of government. And the difficulty was increased by the fact that government, like industry and the professions, presented increasingly the technical and complex problems which the man on the street had no equipment to solve, however well conditioned in the excellent but limited training of the town-hall meeting, which in the eighteenth century had so sturdily developed his ancestors' capacities in the art of self-government. Training so admirably suited for the administration of a small community bore no relation to the needs of a metropolis. The scope of public questions about which the people could have no opinion, on account of their special or technical nature, was constantly enlarging.

Resort to these forms of "direct action"—the initiative, the referendum, and the recall—was symptomatic of the growing distrust of representative government. Such direct popular action has its function. But it cannot take the place of administrative efficiency, because the nature of each is different, and each is limited to the sphere of its competence. A referendum, for instance, is only valuable when it is applied in an area in which a clear opinion can be formed by the voter. It should be confined to questions involving general principles.

If, then, the multitude attempts too much, moves in areas in which it cannot appropriately function, its yoke strangles the freedom and responsiveness of its own institutions. "The plain fact," wrote Lowell, "is that in America democracy undertakes more work, tries to attend to more details for which it is not fitted, than in any other country in the world. . . . The cure for the ills of popular government is more attention by the people to the things they undertake, and that object is not promoted by undertaking too much."[4] Increase in the effectiveness of democracy is not achieved by enlargement of the forms of democratic activity but by insuring the success of a limited but telling participation. Weakening the power of government representatives is not the way to improve their usefulness, which largely depends on making them more responsible.

The increasingly more direct co-operation of the electorate in legislative activities is paralleled by the growth and influence of the lobby. The people are seldom united in a single purpose but are split into minorities whose interests conflict. Manufacturers, farmers, railroad employees, consumers, women, insurance interests, wool-growers—all these have powerful spokesmen to express more directly their desires in the legislative field. Perhaps this cannot be called direct participation of the people in lawmaking, but it is far more direct and far less representative than the legislative structure within which it operates. Play of discretion or exercise of judgment by those elected for the very purpose of exercising it is discarded in favor of more direct guidance transmitted through the lobbyist. The use of the lobby reflects the changed attitude from those days when it was thought enough to have the voters express their preferences, at stated intervals, not in connection with the adoption of any specific measure, but for an individual who, when the time came, would use his own judgment in making the decision on their behalf. The proper display of this function Edmund Burke believed to be the duty of a public man. "Your representative," he wrote in his famous controversy with the electors of Bristol, "owes you, not his industry only, but his judgment; and he betrays, instead of serving you, if he sacrifices it to your opinion."[5] It is said that Lord Macaulay, receiving a letter from one of his constituents which suggested most deferentially that he follow a specific course in connection with some proposed legislation, was profoundly shocked and said so in his answer. How dare this correspondent try to influence his judgment! He had been chosen to act as he thought right, not to follow the commands of others. He spoke angrily, as if someone had attempted to bribe him. Political conceptions have changed since then.

The liberty of the people demanded that the press be free and opinion uncurbed. That freedom was written in the Constitution and has been successfully guarded. The direct effectiveness of the popular will has been enormously increased by a complete freedom of expression.

The license and violence that this freedom sometimes takes have always surprised and puzzled Europeans, accustomed to a press that has never in some countries entirely shaken off censorship and to an intimate and co-operative relationship between government and certain journals which become its official spokesmen. Englishmen are as vigorously opposed to any form of censorship as are Americans. The flare-up of popular opinion in 1947 in England against a suggestion of the Labour government that the press might by some unspecified form of control be made more responsible shows that the British attitude in this respect is similar to ours. Yet they are constantly surprised by the length to which our newspapers are permitted to go. They point out that in their own country the indirect control of the law of libel, with its threat of what seems to us extraordinarily large verdicts rendered by juries and sustained by courts, tends not to curb the expression of any free opinion but to discourage billingsgate and to protect the individual from destructive and unfounded attacks, often irrelevant to the public issue and tending for that reason to confuse rather than to enlighten. To the American temperament, on the other hand, exaggeration of language has always seemed but a normally exuberant expression of life. Our indifference to the dignity of our own institutions is related to the tolerance with which we regard extravagant generalities.

De Tocqueville noted this violence in the first newspaper he read when he landed in the United States in 1831, a young Frenchman not quite twenty-six, sent here by the Minister of Justice to study our prison system. He quotes the following from the *Vincennes Gazette:* "The language of Jackson [the President] has been that of a heartless despot, solely occupied with the preservation of his own authority. . . . Intrigue is his native element. . . . He governs by means of corruption, and his immoral practices will redound to his shame and confusion. His conduct . . . has been that of a shameless and lawless gamester. . . . He will be obliged to disgorge his winnings."[6] We may reflect that the tradition of such unrestraint has not greatly altered but that a certain sales resistance has developed in a public constantly sprayed by the gorgeous language of Hollywood, which dulls the edge and blunts the point of the attacks, so that even editorial writers of such free speakers as the *Chicago Tribune* must at times thumb their *Thesaurus* in search of words not too exhausted under constant driving to convey any critical sense.

The combination of these forces—a political system founded on majority rule, a belief in the value of direct popular participation in that rule, a tradition of equality, emphasis on individual rights, the conviction in and practice of an uncurbed press—creates the enormous influence of public opinion in the United States. The radio has opened a new and compelling means of influencing thought, and the technique of opinion sampling by polls and questionnaires has enabled the harassed statesman to hear with greater distinctness the sound of his master's voice. The immense authority of public opinion in America grows to unlimited proportions as the world shrinks under the impact of new methods of instantaneous communication.

Yet the great mass of citizens do not have the time, the leisure, the objectiveness, or the interest to form any judgment about the myriad problems that are constantly being presented to them. Nor is there any tradition in America, as until recently there still existed in Europe, by which a particular class is looked to for guidance. As often as not, the people do not know what they want. They must count on their public leaders for direction, who in turn seek to find it in that "phantom phrase" public opinion, as evanescent as it is powerful.

If public opinion is the instrument by which democracies must necessarily govern, what happens to the minority under the impact of this domination? Every man can have his say under the law, but will he in fact express himself, assuming, first, that he has the leisure to think and the means to make his thinking effective? His will to independent judgment is constantly sapped by his normal instinct to be submissive. There is safety in numbers. If one assumes, as one must, that in a democracy the decision of the majority must be accepted, the next familiar though mistaken step is to assume that, because made by the majority, the decision must be right. No one likes to disagree with the majority. It is pleasanter, and often wiser for practical considerations, to go along. The belief in right of the majority drifting into the belief that the majority is right creates a "fatalism of the multitude," carrying a sense of the impotence of individual effort, a self-distrust, a disposition to move with the crowd, a "diminished sense of personal responsibility."[7] This fatalistic temper must be expected under a system which assumes social and political equality. It tends to increase under the standardization of mass thinking. But by whatever causes this optimistic yet inert public mind has been created, whether from the quality of our institutions or from the mechanization of our lives, skeptical of its government yet distrustful of individual and original thinking, deeply conservative, vaguely religious yet unreverential, it exists as an immensely conservative and timid force in our daily lives. The strength and fatalism of public opinion make difficult the role and influence of minorities.

We should therefore do everything in our power not only to permit thought that may be upstream but to encourage it. Originality, freshness, and imagination are not applauded in the optimistic cautiousness of American opinion. Qualitative rather than quantitative thinking is rare. Richard Müller-Freienfels, a German professor of psychology and aesthetics, writing in 1927, was of the opinion that quantity in America was not a fact, as in Europe, but a value. The general mechanization of life, the "prevalence of practical thinking" and the "suppression of all that is merely agreeable, emotional, and irrational in the personality,'' the standardization, the mass production, the uniformity, the reduction of individuals to a dead level—these, he believed, were American characteristics. ''Difference, between races and classes and other social groups, and even between individuals . . . uniqueness, and originality are European values, which are foreign to the American. . . . If a thing is untypical it is worthless.''[8]

What I have said does not question the democratic necessity of a strong public opinion or the valuable part that it has played in our history. Nor can any democrat argue against the role of the majority. Generally speaking, with us the majority has not been tyrannous. There are exceptions—the carpet-bagging days that followed the Civil War, white treatment of the Negro minority, and, to some minds at least, the imposition of prohibition. But we have tended, I think, to absorb the role that a minority could play in the huge melting-pot of American life. That role becomes more significant as our future relation to Europe gradually develops.

Little countries in their relation to the great powers are but minorities, and their freedom, too, is at stake. Throughout the world other minorities, not in their proportion to the population where they may be a majority but in their share in government, look for greater freedom and for the outlawing of the discrimination which has set them apart. Two systems are bidding for their allegiance. If the choice is between a free life and one where freedom is abandoned, the reality of the choice may be found in the suggestion of Lord Acton with which I opened this chapter—the amount of security enjoyed by minorities.

The tendency to seek a more direct relation of the people to the exercise of their public affairs and the fatalism of public opinion in America, which limits original thinking, are connected with the American distrust of experts in government.

There is a firmly held bias of the American mind against the use of experts in the public service, a belief that specialists are unnecessary in government, that the people can govern themselves, and that it is all a matter of sound judgment, not technical knowledge or experience. The social revolution which elected Andrew Jackson to the presidency carried this implication into the philosophy of the spoils system and rotation in office.

Lowell makes the interesting suggestion that the principle of rotation in office was based not only on the philosophy that to the victor belong the spoils but on "the feeling that a new man, coming fresh from the people, will be in closer touch with popular opinion and will be free from official habits, or, in other words, a fairer sample of the public. This is the reason that jurymen serve short periods and are constantly replaced by a fresh panel." The purpose of drawing a jury by lot is to insure mediocrity, "for impartiality could be secured, as in the case of judges, by other means." Choice by lot and rotation in office was the basis of Greek city government and was regarded by Aristotle and his contemporaries as essentially democratic. It was freely used in Venice in the election of the doge.[9]

Rotation in office was not too unsuited to American agrarian civilization when any conception of government beyond one which would keep order and apply the most rudimentary social laws seemed to interfere with the "manifest destiny" of the people. But it is obviously mischievous when applied to the intricate complexities of the modern state.

Lowell concludes his study of public opinion and government with these words: "Whether popular government will endure or not depends upon its success in solving its problems, and among these none is more insistent than the question of its capacity both to use and to control experts, a question closely interwoven with the nature, the expression, and the limitations of public opinion."[10]

Today that is even more true. I think that it may be fairly said of our more recent development that the need of experts in the work of government, as that work is continually expanded in every field of service, has at last begun to be generally realized. A politician is trained essentially in the layman's outlook; he has been developed to understand and respond to the average mind, to group psychology, to share the attitude of the mass, to feel the emotions of the public. Skilful in grasping and manipulating these interests and adjustments, he is not alert or responsive to the need of special skills and trained knowledge. But of recent years increasingly the politician has been forced to turn to the expert.

In the foreign field our lack of experts is particularly noticeable at this time. This situation is the result of many causes; some recent, some reaching far back into our early history. That in a large sense the country never had a foreign policy for many years accounts to some extent for the inadequacy of our present available personnel. Nor is our contemptuous attitude toward government, even our own, calculated to attract first-rate men to public service. And the fact, as Geoffrey Gorer, a British anthropologist, has suggested, that Americans regard their government as alien and fail to identify themselves with it makes unlikely any feeling of joint responsibility.[11] The result is that those who administer a policy, particularly in the foreign field, often feel themselves suspect and become timid under the constant fear of offending public opinion. Ultimately administration shapes the policy, and the public suffers from a sense of frustration because they cannot achieve what they have chosen. The result is a sense of confusion when we see our foreign policies in operation. Senator Richard Russell, after a journey through the Mediterranean, reported to his colleagues on October 28, 1943: "The British have a definite foreign policy with respect to every corner of the globe. Every civil servant and every officer of rank is apparently fully acquainted with Empire policy. . . . If our Nation has a definite policy which extends longer than six months after the conclusion of the war . . . I was unable to find anyone among our officers abroad who could define it."[12]

The public does not adequately realize that the expression of the will of the majority is not enough if it is not translated into effective action on the level of administration. The people must learn to depend on their experts—and, to a far greater extent, to let them alone.

It would be a mistake to stress our need for using experts in government unless we emphasize, as did Lowell, that we must control as well as use them. Experts essentially belong to the line whose function is technical and advisory and whose duties are to inform the staff before the campaign has been planned and to put it into operation after the staff has made the decision. Special training and knowledge is not usually a requirement we should look for in a top administrator. The heads of our war and navy departments have usually been laymen, exercising their broader experience in general affairs over the narrower and more specialized outlook of their subordinates. The place of the "generalist" in public life is as important as that of the specialist, but their functions must not be confused.

Finally, we must never forget that public opinion should be led as well as followed. If one test of our democracy is the ability to use experts, another is to fulfil our instinctive need for greatness by choosing men to guide the direction of our destiny who can stir the timid and sluggish caution of the multitude with the vision of great horizons.

V

THE WORD "DEMOCRACY": TYRANNY OF GOVERNMENT, FREEDOM OF THE INDIVIDUAL

✼

IN ANY growing and vital social organism rights are not static and for that reason can never be bound by the limitations of minute definition. As the increasing insistence on equality grew out of our Colonial society, which, though organized in its language, law, and cultural outlook on British institutions, had never fully accepted the inherited class arrangements that characterized the older country, it became obvious that the ambitions of individual men, each considering himself as good as the next, would soon produce vigorous and often bitter clashes with those arrangements. A man's freedom obviously cannot be absolute but is limited by the competing interests of others and the demands of the community as a whole. To secure the rights of "life, liberty, and the pursuit of happiness," government, so says our Declaration, is "instituted among men." A referee is chosen to settle disputes. And in American institutions, political as well as athletic, the referee, from the Founding Fathers down to the World Series, has ever been regarded by all good citizens with skepticism, suspicion, and hostility. His decisions must ultimately be accepted, for that is a rule without which the game cannot be played. But he remains a fair target for any missile and can always be fired and another referee chosen who will have the sense not to favor one side only.

For, after all, he is *our* referee.

Thus runs a deep-seated American instinct. Distrust of the government, a natural corollary to belief in the sovereignty of the people, underlies the federal Constitution. Everywhere power is checked and dispersed. The functions of government are distributed between two sovereigns. The states must not impinge on the central government and are protected from aggression by it. The legislative is balanced against the executive, the judiciary marshaled against both. Individuals are surrounded with safeguards against actions by their new sovereigns. Into some fields neither sovereign must ever move. This adjustment of functions to insure against their misuse appears not only in the federal Constitution but in the constitutions of the states, on which the former was largely modeled. The men who framed the Constitution of the United States were determined that they would never again be subjected to the tyranny of a sovereign, for were not all sovereigns, given unchecked power, bound to be tyrannous? The Declaration which they had finally made, after solemn thought and grave misgivings, was an indictment of the tyranny of George the Third.

Above all else these men distrusted authority.

Many of the checks and balances are also the result of compromise, for the same outlook which led the framers to be cautious in granting strength to the new federal agencies made the smaller states afraid that authority might be abused by the greater. If Hobbes and Locke had taught the delegates the belief that power belongs to the people and must, if it is to be retained by the people, be widely scattered among the branches of government, Calvin's gloomy view of human nature was not without influence on their minds. Puritanism, like the Mormon church, was a political theory as well as a religious doctrine. The Constitution, says Bryce, "is the work of men

who believed in original sin, and were resolved to leave open
for transgressors no door which they could possibly shut,"
quoting, in support, Chief Justice Marshall's remark, in his
Life of Washington, that because "power might be abused was
deemed a conclusive reason why it should not be conferred."[1]
We find in these beginnings, therefore, the role of government
conceived as limited and negative—half-policeman, half-ref-
eree, with emphasis on the former's function of keeping order
rather than on the latter's of settling disputes. This conception
was to change, as all theories gradually yield to the tougher
persuasion of facts, to that of a much more comprehensive
part for the state to play, as new problems demanded new
solutions. But in 1787 the government was not thought of as
positive, certainly not as "a great ideal power, capable of
guiding and developing a nation's life."[2]

The assumption that government is in itself tyrannous, and
we should therefore have as little of it as possible, is still a
part of the folklore of our politicians and of a majority of our
people, for the public men, who know what they are about,
would not talk that way if there was no instinctive sympathetic response. Because this view is closely allied to our traditional devotion to laissez faire, it is often expressed in another form, hardly consistent with the first but equally a part
of the American myth. Government—so the legend runs—particularly when contrasted to individual initiative, is weak and
inefficient; so, the less government, the better. Obversely, the
tendency of all rulers has been to usurp power. To keep them
under control, they must be stripped of all activities except
those necessary for strictly limited functioning. Therefore, all
but minimal functions should be privately exercised. The two
theories have instinctively interlocked in a defensive embrace.

It is interesting and curious to note, even as public activities
increase and the resources of our government are used more

and more comprehensively across the world, that many of our distinguished business and professional leaders repeat with earnest if perhaps naïve emphasis their sincere conviction of the lamentable failure of their own public institutions. A half-dozen years ago, for instance, Philip B. Reed, chairman of the board of directors of the General Electric Company, expressed this attitude in what he called a primer of American government, spread in a full-page advertisement in the *Saturday Evening Post:* "Remember that Government belongs to the people, is inherently inefficient, and that its activities should be limited to those which Government alone can perform." Mr. Justice Frankfurter quotes the words of a former president of the United States Chamber of Commerce: "The best public servant is the worst one. . . . A thoroughly first-rate man in public service is corrosive. He eats holes in our liberties. The better he is and the longer he stays the greater is the danger"[3]—on the hypothesis, presumably, that, since government is bound to be incompetent, its officials should preferably be mediocre. And, finally, this is what one of America's most successful lawyers, a former United States senator, had to say at a dinner of the American Bar Association in 1940: "What Government *has* is only what these men and women can in the name of Government take by taxation and borrowing from those who have the ability and energy to do in industry what they themselves cannot do. What Government *does*, therefore, is in this way to appropriate the resources of the competent, thus preventing them from wisely directing and controlling the flow of their own capital, and instead to entrust that vital function to the incompetent." Added up, these pronouncements of three of our most respected citizens amount to this: Government, inherently inefficient and preferably mediocre, employs the incompetent to waste the resources of the able and the energetic. And, remember, they are not attacking a particular government, that of Franklin Delano Roosevelt, for instance, but "government" in general. The shibboleth is very ancient. Had not, indeed, Plato once described democracy as "a charming form of government, full of variety and disorder, and dispensing a kind of equality to equals and unequals alike"?[4]

The credo of laissez faire, which "as a social concept reached complete logical development in American courts, just as it was breaking down as a social structure before modern industrialism,"[5] although interfering with did not stop the growth of public activity in every field, throughout every administration, by nation and states alike. The political pattern is almost fixed. An administration that is in adopts laws to protect farmers, shippers, children at work, investors, the old and the unemployed. It is attacked by those who are out as being tyrannous, as breaking down individual initiative pampering the idle, destroying the "American way." Yet the people, although theoretically accepting laissez faire as a flattering economic theory, if theory it can be called, insist, as their needs increase and the consciousness of their power grows, on the adoption of the laws they think will better their lives. And when the political change comes, and the critics of those measures now must administer them, more laws are added, more administrative agencies set up, and it is the turn of their opponents, now out, to challenge the sacrilege that is being done to the temple of free enterprise. Under his chapter on laissez faire, Bryce, writing over forty years ago, instances many examples of state protective legislation. "The farmer of Kansas or Iowa," he remarks, "is more palpably the object of the paternal solicitude of his legislature than the farmer of any European country."[6] Socialistic? Heaven forbid! For surely the western farmer is a rugged individualist if ever there was one. But farmers, like manufacturers, railroads, and merchants, turned increasingly to their government to advance their own immediate and practical ends.

What once is branded as socialism finally becomes an accepted commonplace American institution. In arguing against the income-tax law of 1894, before the United States Supreme Court, Joseph H. Choate described it as "communistic in its purposes and tendencies and is here defended upon principles as communistic, socialistic—what shall I call them—populistic as have ever been addressed to any political assembly in the world!"[7] When Bryan included postal savings in his platform in 1896, he was denounced as advocating socialism; but that did not prevent President Taft, a few years later, from signing without protest a postal savings bill.

It is hard to say when the changed outlook was first reflected in definite expression and the belief advanced that the state should be used to serve its people. By the time of the Civil War, Samuel E. Morison notes, "the Union, which for Washington was a justification for the American Revolution, and for Hamilton a panoply of social order, had become, in the hands of Jackson, Clay, and Webster, a symbol of popular government."[8] "We believe that the government, like every other intelligent agency," Horace Greeley, the editor of the *New York Tribune*, wrote before the Civil War, "is bound to do good to the extent of its ability—that it ought actively to promote and increase the general well-being." Karl Marx had been writing for the *Tribune* in the forties.[9] Theodore Roosevelt hated socialism and said so; but, in the opinion of the Beards, he "was the first President of the United States who openly proposed to use the powers of political government for the purpose of affecting the distribution of wealth in the interest of the golden mean." Writing to Jacob Riis, in 1906, Roosevelt voiced his intention, "so far as it can be done by legislation, to favor the growth of intelligence and the diffusion of wealth in such a manner as will measurably avoid the extreme of swollen fortunes and grinding poverty."[10]

The most striking recent example of the extent to which the people of the United States are using their government to serve their needs is the Tennessee Valley Authority. The objects of the act which authorized its creation in 1935 were unified river control—flood control and navigability and the generation and sale of electric power, the manufacture and sale of fertilizer, and the agricultural and industrial development of the Tennessee Valley. Such an undertaking in private hands would have been impossible. It was a new experiment in an almost unknown and untried field, the development of a whole region which from deforestation, floods, and erosion had become submarginal. The region was bounded not by the artificial lines of state or county but by boundaries determined by the need for finding an integrated solution of a common problem. The Tennessee Valley was such an area, within which the unco-ordinated branches of government—national, state, and local—were brought together in a successful voluntary co-operation, a co-operation which, said the congressional committee which investigated the operation of the Authority in 1938–39, had strengthened "the confidence of the people in their own democratic institutions."[11] The undertaking was bitterly fought. Attempts were made by its opponents to destroy it in the courts and to discredit it with the people. The attempts failed. The experiment was so obviously successful, after a few years of operation, that now T.V.A. is generally accepted. The state was servicing the people. Political theory yielded to practical demands.

The dualism in the American nature between private theory and public practice is puzzling to the foreign observer. It is the ancient contradiction between symbol and reality, between what we say and what we do. The inconsistency underlies the functioning of all society. I do not suggest that this contradiction so often mistaken for hypocrisy, which it is not, is more characteristic of American nature, of Anglo-Saxon thinking, than of the Latin or Oriental. Are the French more consistent? Do their actions more closely reflect the temper of their thinking, of their national folklore? I do not know. The dualism puzzles our neighbors, most of whom are more advanced in the use of the service state than are we, and who cannot understand our ritualistic opposition to public measures which we accept whenever it suits our convenience.

If, for instance, they look into our actions to see to what extent they square with our belief in competition as the ultimate good, they will note that the belief was expressed in the broadest possible terms nearly sixty years ago in the famous Sherman Antitrust Act. *Every* combination in restraint of interstate commerce was declared illegal. The ideal which lay at the very heart of the American tradition, the tough unyielding belief in free enterprise as the best way of living, was written into law. Yet, year after year, combinations which eliminated competition flourished and increased in size and number, with the operations of the law occasionally dislocating them on paper, so that the net effect was more to suggest new methods of evasion than to challenge their growth or dominance. Again the theory and the practice. . . . If you write down your principles on paper, neatly wrap them up in a law, you feel free to practice as you will, to prove that mere behavior cannot tarnish the principles, which are eternal, and you lead the luxury of a double life, keeping your moral cake and eating up your competitors. In the Introduction to their book *Cartels in Action*, Stocking and Watkins thus note the difference between the philosophy of competition and its current practice: "The assumptions of unhindered initiation of productive enterprise, of unobstructed flow of investment funds . . . of single-minded preoccupation . . . with cost reduction and sales expansion, and of unmitigated rivalry for patronage—

with the humble consumer in the enviable position of the biblical meek—these assumptions are the gist of the folklore by which businessmen keep alive their faith in the current economic system. . . . What was once a way of life in the business world is fast becoming a way of rumination—or oratory. If competition is to survive, it must be more than a shibboleth or a slogan. The discrepancy between the truths which men live by—in business—and the truths which they profess but do not live by, is one of the most significant, and disturbing, revelations of this survey."[12]

Harry A. Bullis, president of General Mills, Incorporated, speaking at the company's nineteenth annual stockholders' meeting on August 19, 1947, is reported to have said during the course of his protest against recent antitrust suits: "These attacks on the free working of our system must be resisted; they are tantamount to sabotage of our early return to an ordered and balanced economy."[13]

Thurman Arnold's vivid enforcement of the Sherman Act was hardly, to put it mildly, popular among the rank and file of American businessmen. . . .

This dualism, inherent in the American temperament, is a conflict not only between the ideal and the practical but between the "note of personal independence that was, and in the main still is, dominant in American life" and the friendly dependence inherited from the pioneer days in the wilderness when a man turned to his neighbor for help. "Hence the dual nature of the American: individualism and herd instinct, indifference and kindliness, a combination so puzzling to longer established peoples."[14] The conflict continually presents nice problems of political judgment. In which direction will the average man respond to any given stimulus? If social legislation is popular, filling his deep-rooted approval of community effort, it is a risk to attack the program which it expresses and wiser to level your aim at those who have sponsored and administered the laws rather than the laws themselves.

The assumed effectiveness if not the accuracy of the ancient slogans has recently been revived by our strained relations with the U.S.S.R. during the last two years. The battle cry that New Dealers were Communists had become a little shopworn in presidential elections. But now American Communists, who had previously been thought of by some of us as a pest, were suddenly discovered by most of us to be a menace. Leaders of both parties realized the potentialities of the situation about the same time—perhaps communism would be or could be made to be the issue for 1948—and rushed in to seize and wave the flag, fearlessly beating the tomtoms, a little breathless, their brows wrinkled with the disturbing thought that their opponents might reach the band wagon first. Businessmen, tasting the heady wine which the statesmen had drunk, began to draw red circles around those who disagreed with them. Their thinking, if not clear, was beautifully simple. The executive vice-president of the National Association of Real Estate Boards solemnly declared, in a speech before the Thirty-eighth Annual Convention of the Ohio Association of Real Estate Boards, that Senator Taft, who had sponsored the rather mild Taft-Ellender-Wagner Public Housing Bill, stood "for socialism in housing, in medicine and in general welfare"—public housing which he characterized as "the basic step of all Communistic programs, the most persuasive form of demagogery politicians ever found."[15]

I have suggested emphasis on the individual, on equality, and on laissez faire as central themes in the American heritage. Yet, as no right is absolute, particularly in a new and aggressive society, no theory of government can be absolutely applied without qualification, and there is compromise between the theory and the aspects of particular problems as they arise. If "the state and society were nothing; the individual . . .

everything," and "government intervention was an evil, a violation of the inexorable laws of nature,"[16] how explain the increasing responsibilities which this feeble and despised instrument of government was asked to assume? Besides the obvious answer that no theory can be pushed to its logical extreme, it must be remembered that the cult of unrestrained capitalism, sanctifying its harsh logic to a moral dogma, disregarded in practice the certain reaction which its rigid application was bound to create. Human beings cared more for economic well-being than for the "moral" law which they were told created it. The "law" had indeed never prevented those who most piously invoked it from using the government— which must never interfere—from building tariff walls, donating public land to railroads, and subsidizing the owners of ships.

Yet to realize that in practice the doctrine of free enterprise was often not followed is not to deny that the most central of the themes—emphasis on the individual—is the *sine qua non* of the democratic outlook. The problem, essentially of degree, is the use to which government should be put in the effort to achieve the greatest possible freedom and happiness for human beings. There cannot be complete agreement on this; there must be compromise, particularly where the immense flow of new invention and industrial expansion continually renews the contest.

In general, those who dislike change, who inherit a sense of history, who distrust the ever growing tendency of the state to increase its functions, are called conservatives and, in holding to the past, often tend to overemphasize the axioms which in their fathers' day held greater reality than when applied to contemporary needs. The radicals, or progressives as they have more recently come to be known—I do not use the word to suggest extremists—believe that fundamental changes in the structure of society are called for and usually look to their elected agents, loosely thought of as "government," to achieve the desired ends. They are more tempted to yield to the magic illusion of change and to believe that environment, and hence human nature, can be altered by the discriminating application of legislation and a greater use of political power. I avoid the use of "liberal" to describe the attitude of mind opposed to the conservative, because the word "liberal," though often today used in that sense, seems to me to define more exactly a mind whose primary interest is planted in the soil of toleration, in the give-and-take of free movements, whether in thought or in the market place. Thus thought of, a liberal may be conservative or radical. The late Mr. Justice Holmes was certainly a thoroughgoing liberal in this sense. Although he distrusted much of the contemporary effort to "improve" the world by legislation, and accepted the teachings of Adam Smith and of Malthus as a conservative would accept the thought which was current at the time of his youth, he believed to the marrow of his bones in the value of the free play of ideas and the importance of permitting them to find expression in legislative experiment. "But when men have realized that time has upset many fighting faiths," he wrote in one of his great dissents, "they may come to believe even more than they believe the very foundations of their own conduct that the ultimate good desired is better reached by free trade in ideas—that the best test of truth is the power of the thought to get itself accepted in the competition of the market, and that truth is the only ground upon which their wishes safely can be carried out."[17]

Men may roughly be divided into these two groups, with various shades and limitations. Yet they are likely to discard their inherited tradition when unemployment, or some other fundamental dislocation of their routine, makes them skeptical of eternal values and turns their faces toward any new star if only it seems to illumine the solution of the immediate and the pressing.

Since the opposition of these two points of view in American business and political life is more clear-cut and more violent than the mild differences that separate the two parties, men shift from one to another at elections, interested in getting things politically done or undone. Party policies and principles, as has so often been observed, are frequently indistinguishable. The platforms are generally vague and avoid issues, and the campaign speeches are singularly alike and rather colorless except for a certain amount of expected vituperation. Everyone is counted on to call names—is almost judged in this great national sport by his skill in doing so. The parties do not face the issues. Small groups of men within the parties, in the Senate or House, often crossing party lines, now and then a state governor who has the courage to say something and do something—Charles Evans Hughes, Alfred E. Smith, Ellis Arnall—or an occasional vigorous President—Theodore Roosevelt, Woodrow Wilson, Franklin Roosevelt—define and express the inarticulate needs of the people. Whether expressed through movements cutting across party lines, as with us, or, as in Great Britain, through parties which more nearly represent this fundamental difference between conservative and radical, the play of these two forces is vital to the health and growth of democratic institutions. Each point of view has its place in the American theme. To say, therefore, that he who would increase the area of government activities is a Communist, and hence un-American, is neither true nor at this particular moment wise, for the remark falls strangely on foreign ears, unaccustomed to the repetition of such political catch-words, which we have learned to take half-seriously, or indeed to disregard, particularly as a presidential election approaches.

This is a theme which I shall develop more fully in a subsequent chapter. I wish to indicate here, however, that the doctrine of individualism, so essentially American, neither is clear in our own minds nor has it guided our activities in the practical operations of government. Our system of "free" competitive enterprise certainly does not mean freedom from state control and regulation; and it can be called competitive only in a guarded and conditional sense. In large segments of American industry competition is unknown; in others it is regulated by economic power unrelated to any activity of government; in still others the "laws" of competition have comparatively free play. Our economy has changed from individual production to mass production; from individual ownership to the anonymous title of paper shares in the mass property; from an individual to a managerial capitalism. Certainly this is not state socialism. But is it any more accurate to call it "individual enterprise"?

Lewis L. Lorwin has coined the word "neocapitalism" to describe a thesis having its roots in the work of John Maynard Keynes, who believed that laissez faire cannot any longer insure economic security or political freedom. The power of great corporations and organized economic groups has eliminated the free market and "has changed the process of price-making." Neocapitalism is based on private enterprise but proposes that "the government undertake to guarantee reasonably full employment and to police the competitive process in such a way that a new type of 'free market' will result." The program includes extensive social security "and public provisions for better housing, nutrition, schools, and health."[18] It would seem to be supported by a large body of opinion and to describe in a general way the kind of economy that has been developing in America since the depression began in 1929. Certainly the economy of laissez faire, though saluted by the platforms of all political parties, is not sustained by the particular planks of which those platforms are built.

Individualism as an economic doctrine, it would seem, is hardly susceptible of definition and even less of practical application. It is scarcely more than a point of view which has greatly influenced our development, but it cannot be said to be the actual basis of our society. Fear and contempt of government, so characteristic of much American sentiment, is alien to the traditions of western European society. Europeans are less likely than we to fear the difficulties of government and to overestimate the average man. They inherit a greater respect for the dignity and honor implied in public service. They are less given to abstractions so dear to the American heart. Their institutions have been developed gradually in ancient and closely knit communities. Their thinking is not shaped by the American experience of pioneer life in a recent past. They do not believe that salvation can be achieved only from the unrestrained play of the laws of competition. The idea of planning shocks no prejudice in their minds, even if planning be on a public level.

Laissez faire, in short, cannot be included in those definite rights, clearly outlined, simply apprehended, which are at the core of any democratic system. It should not be classed among the basic freedoms of Western civilization which, it would appear, we are committed to defend. These rights and freedoms I shall examine in the next chapter.

VI

THE ESSENTIAL RIGHTS

✲

THE dualism in the American temperament of which I
have spoken—the vigorous instinct to be let alone by government which is continually in conflict with the longing to
find expression in community effort, coupled with a pragmatic
outlook that discards theory for the solution of the immediate
need—makes it difficult to define "the American way." We
can say with assurance, however, that most Americans will
agree that it involves the conviction that the individual must
never be subordinated to the state and that he must be protected from state domination by institutions which experience
has shown to be necessary to insure ultimate control of their
governments by the people. Discussion of political abstractions is less fruitful than an examination of the nature of those
institutions.

We find in the Constitution and Bill of Rights, in our laws
and our practices, definite and explicit affirmations of our theory of democratic government. Most of them are so much a
part of our everyday life that we fail to remember how long a
struggle in the history of mankind took place—indeed, in the
history of our own country—before they could be achieved.
We had always assumed that in Europe, as with us, even in
countries of the Old World which we thought of as less democratic than our own, a minimum of political rights was preserved. Then we saw Hitler's ruthless imperialism destroy
those rights—boastfully preaching that they were soft and
outmoded—while he conquered and held, tortured and en-

slaved, a very substantial part of the world. When he was defeated, we felt that we had helped preserve our way of living, threatened from the outside, no longer sheltered behind a sea. And now we find, in these years of cold struggle, that under the impact of a not dissimilar imperialism, with the same techniques of conquest, seizure of "friendly" controlled governments, mass deportations and enslavements, and the same control and concentration of propaganda, such rights as existed in eastern Europe are not merely threatened but have been destroyed. They might, almost overnight, disappear, too, in western Europe. It is natural, therefore, that we should take a look at our own civil liberties in order to determine the extent to which we have sustained them as realities in our country, now that we are committed to give them the type of economic environment abroad from which they might suck enough sustenance to live. As a wave of reaction and "liberal baiting" swept the country, greater interest at the same time developed in championing these liberties. The admirable report of the President's Committee on Civil Rights, to which I have already referred, was one of the results.

Protection of civil rights stems from the original Constitution. The checks and balances and distribution of powers shield the individual against government tyranny. An ancient abuse of the sovereign, now almost forgotten, the raising of revenues without the consent of the legislature, is forbidden, and all revenue bills are made to originate in the House of Representatives, whose members are directly elected by the people every two years. Neither the federal government nor any state shall pass "any bill of attainder or *ex post facto* law." The privilege of the ancient writ of habeas corpus cannot be suspended except in cases of rebellion or invasion. Crimes must be tried by jury in the state in which they are committed.

The people elect their executives and legislatures at regular stated intervals.

This was the original outline, such were the guaranties of the Constitution before amendment, guaranties based on the expensive lessons of history. But they were not enough. The first ten amendments (Bill of Rights), protecting individuals against national encroachment, were added two years later. The amendments guaranteeing civil liberties are the first: freedom of religion, of speech, and of the press, and the right to assemble peaceably and to petition the government to redress grievances; the fourth: forbidding unreasonable searches and seizures; the fifth: providing for grand-jury indictments, against double jeopardy and self-incrimination, for due process of law, and for compensation for private property taken for public use; the sixth: directing speedy and public trial by an impartial jury of the state and district where the crime is committed and giving the accused the right to be informed of the nature of the accusation, to be confronted with the witnesses against him, and to obtain witnesses and have counsel for his defense; and the eighth: preventing excessive bail or fines or the imposition of cruel and unusual punishment.

Here are definite and specific fundamentals, the enforcement of which should preserve the people from the destruction of their liberties. Free opinion, fair trials, regular elections—are not these the tests of the democratic state?

I suspect that we are sometimes likely to believe that all our rights flow from the Constitution itself. We have the nostalgic reverence of a pioneer people for concepts formally declared and inscribed, as if the act of writing made them eternal and hence unchangeable. It is a great instrument, and it is fitting that we should revere it. Yet many of our rights flow not from the Constitution but from legislation and can be destroyed by the repeal of the laws that create them.

None of these original constitutional rights have been abandoned. The Civil War amendments extended the rights of citizens to the newly emancipated Negroes. Other rights, not found in the basic document, have gradually been accepted as essential to the exercise of the freedoms guaranteed by it. The right to collective bargaining, nowhere suggested in the Constitution, since 1935 is guaranteed by law and accepted, at least in theory, by the public. The secret ballot is now generally considered necessary to protect the independence of the electorate in voting. Yet the first secret-ballot law was not passed until a hundred years after the Constitution had been adopted; and twenty years later seven states had not enacted such legislation, although in three (Mississippi, Texas, Kentucky) provisions for the secret ballot had been embodied in the state constitutions. By 1936 "Australian ballot" laws were in force in all the states except Delaware, Georgia, and South Carolina. Delaware still permits the distribution of ballots prior to the election. Under a law adopted in 1922 Georgia authorized counties, through two successive grand juries, to use secret voting. And, although the supreme court of South Carolina has ruled that balloting must be secret, it has accepted as a satisfactory practice the distribution of ballots at the voting place.[1]

Civil service legislation has gradually been enacted by the federal government, the states, and most municipalities. And with the acceptance of civil service has grown the idea that civil servants have a "right" to be shielded from arbitrary dismissal. Of course, no such right exists under the Constitution and is found only in the civil service laws. Yet to many believers in the American tradition it came as a shock that this right should have been so casually abrogated in 1947 in the rider to the State Department appropriation law, allowing, in substance, the Secretary of State to discharge employees without stating the reasons or granting any administrative review or appeal. As to this the President's Committee says: "Accordingly, provision should be made for such traditional procedural safeguards as the right to a bill of particular accusations, the right to subpoena witnesses and documents where genuine security considerations permit, the right to be represented by counsel, the right to a stenographic report of proceedings, the right to a written decision, and the right of appeal."[2]

The concept of the democratic state that governments are instituted by *men* to secure the rights of *men* underlies the committee's report. To three basic rights: "Safety and Security of the Person," "Citizenship and Its Privileges," and "Freedom of Conscience and Expression," the committee adds a fourth: "The Right to Equality of Opportunity." It is a right nowhere found in the Constitution and, before the second World War, hardly conceived of in the legal sense as being susceptible of definition and enforcement under statutory authority. We had almost accepted discrimination until the war dramatized the gross unfairness which tolerated its existence and emphasized its corrupting effect on our society. Its evils came to the surface under the pressure of war demands and the scarcity of manpower. Now, as Walter White recently remarked, discrimination is no longer fashionable. The committee recommends that laws be enacted by the states prohibiting discrimination in education, in housing, and in the operation of public utilities and health facilities. "In a democracy, each individual must have freedom to choose his friends and to control the pattern of his personal and family life. But we see nothing inconsistent between this freedom and a recognition of the truth that democracy also means that in going to school, working, participating in the political process, serving in the armed forces, enjoying government services in such fields as health and recreation, making use of transportation and other public accommodation facilities, and living in specific communities and neighborhoods, distinction of race, color, and creed have no place."

The committee's assignment was to determine what improvements could be made "to safeguard the civil rights of the people." They did not, therefore, evaluate the extent to which civil rights had been achieved or strike a balance sheet of progress and shortcomings. Progress they found and also that "there has never been a time when the American people have doubted the validity of . . . the ideals of freedom and equality." The committee called attention to the steady decline in the last two decades in the number of lynchings but added that "there has not yet been a year in which America has been completely free of the crime of lynching. . . . The pervasive gap between our aims and what we actually do is creating a kind of moral dry rot which eats away at the emotional and rational bases of democratic beliefs."[3]

The gap must be narrowed in a world in which the masses are revolting against subjugation of the spirit by the cruel application of a double standard. We cannot any longer expect acceptance of a democratic faith by others if we ourselves do not practice it. Every lynching in the war, every instance of mob violence, the race riots in Detroit, were fuel to German and Japanese propaganda. It is sad, therefore, as Congress adopts the program for the recovery of Europe, to see United States senators and governors of southern states attack the President's civil rights message, based on his committee's report, and fulminate against the principles of American democracy that are carved deep in our Declaration and in our Constitution. It is no answer to say that this was to be expected from the history of the South, where state legislation, before the Civil War, had made criticism of slavery a criminal offense. Nor is it enough that conditions are slowly and gradually improving. All over the world men and women watch what we do, listen to what we say. But they listen also to the voice of the Soviets, who smile and point to the American senators and governors and broadcast their words for everyone to hear.

I have elsewhere pointed out that those who drafted our Constitution feared more than anything else the tyranny of government and translated much of their fear into that document. Robert K. Carr finds the same tradition in our attitude to our civil rights. "The American has been inclined to regard the state itself as the great enemy of civil liberty." Today we begin to realize that government can also be a friend to that liberty, "both a shield and a sword," to use Mr. Justice Jackson's graphic phrase. The shield is the "negative safeguard" of invalidating state or federal action that interferes with the individual rights guaranteed by the Constitution. The sword is the positive weapon of criminal action which the state uses against violators of those rights. The proposed federal anti-lynching bill is an effort to sharpen the "sword" of the federal government. It is significant that the role of the state is today conceived of in both capacities. Mr. Justice Murphy, when as Attorney-General he organized the Civil Rights Section of the Department of Justice in 1939, stated: "In a democracy, an important function of the law enforcement branch of government is the aggressive protection of fundamental rights inherent in a free people." A committee of the American Law Institute in its "Statement of Essential Human Rights" emphasizes this positive role for the state. "The State has a duty to protect this freedom" is a clause applied to most of the rights enumerated. "The duty of the State . . . involves," the Committee asserts, "some or all of the following steps: (1) to abstain from enacting laws which impair the right; (2) to prevent its governmental agencies and officials from performing acts which impair the right; (3) to enact laws and provide suitable procedures, if necessary, to prevent persons within its jurisdiction from impairing the right; and (4) to maintain such judicial, regulatory and operative agencies as may be necessary to give practical effect to the right." Since "government has traditionally been regarded as the villain in the civil rights drama," threats from other sources have been until recently disregarded.[4] Laws intended to prevent religious and racial discrimination in employment, now enacted in several states, and the recommendation of similar legislation by the President's Committee, indicate the growing belief that the protection of individual civil rights is a responsibility of government.

Our constitutional and statutory "rights" fall into two classes: the substantive satisfactions which, it is deemed, all men and women should enjoy and the political institutions calculated to insure their enjoyment. Examples of the first are freedom of religious worship and the right to collective bargaining. These two instances illustrate the growth in our conception of the fundamental satisfactions which the state should protect. This is not the place to consider which rights are "natural," and therefore, according to "natural law," may not be abrogated by the state, and which, state-created, may be removed by the state, without violating the moral considerations which are said to inhere in "natural" rights. It is clear, however, that certain of them are more generally considered fundamental than others. Religious liberty, for instance, has deeper roots in our consciousness than freedom to bargain collectively.

In the second class—rights which are instrumental—fall such political institutions as courts, regular elections, and trial by jury. The classification, however, does not satisfy us in determining which rights are intrinsic and as ultimate as anything can be. The three essential freedoms—to worship freely, to speak freely, to assemble freely—without which the integrity of the individual cannot be achieved, are surely fundamental to any form of democracy. That they are not absolute does not make them any less basic. We must stand on them, wherever our influence may tell. Charles E. Merriam, cutting to the root, believes that all rights stem from one "basic human right, common to all humanity . . . the right to live, the right to the fullest and finest development of the potentialities of the human personality in the framework of the common good . . . the recognition of the innate dignity of man."[5] We said in our Declaration that among "certain unalienable rights" are "life, liberty, and the pursuit of happiness." It is less important to try to classify them—civil, political, economic, social—or to test them by a yardstick of constitutional or statutory expression than to remember that the democratic faith must affirm the individual's right to live a free life. In the modern world economic well-being will probably be included in that definition.

The instrumental rights are but means to an end, and it is always more difficult to obtain agreement on the methods by which such ideals may be achieved than to share the ultimate desire for freedom and security. Men do not differ so much in their aspirations for happiness and peace. They soon fall apart in trying to settle on the steps they think necessary to attain them. A Latin would doubtless agree on the importance of a nonpolitical judicial system. Yet he might not share our enthusiasm for trial by jury, imbedded in our Constitution, which he perhaps would consider a clumsy and unscientific method of arriving at the truth. The theory of criminal conspiracy, which played such a large part at the first Nuremberg trial, was alien to the French members of the tribunal, who considered that such a "loose" conception violated an individual right fundamental to European jurisprudence—that the charge of a crime should be concrete and precise. What to us would appear a matter of form and degree may become to the Latin one of substance and principle. But that differences will arise in considering rights of this type does not mean that their recognition is not necessary, for without the instrumental rights the substantive satisfactions would soon cease to exist.

Americans, it has been observed, tend to translate their national views of politics, of morals, or of policy into universal laws and ethical absolutes which, since they have appeared to work in the United States, must be applicable to Europe. Geoffrey Gorer believes that for Americans European countries are rated according to their approximation to America and that to them "taking part in an international undertaking means extending American activities outside the boundaries of the United States."[6]

We should not insist that other nations, finding their democratic path, adopt instruments of government modeled on our own Constitution. Surely the first consideration, in this new world policy, is that governments be genuinely free rather than they be democratic. We do not bring pressure on the republics of Latin America to use American democratic institutions as models. Why should we apply our standards to the particular needs of other peoples or assume that institutions which have worked for us should for that reason satisfy them?

Yet there is a core of rights on which Americans and Europeans can agree and about which democrats the world over will not greatly differ. Such agreement is important, for the democratic ideal in a world that is divided in its political belief must be expressed in comparatively simple terms and sustained in some unity of faith. To us the approach will be in the familiar language of our Constitution; to Europeans, in terms which reaffirm the value and the reality of their own ways of living. There will be diversity of view in emphasis, in means, and particularly in those matters which involve the relation of the individual to the state. I believe, however, that the general principles on which agreement can be reached can be summarized in a line or two: Men must be allowed to elect and control their government—free and regular elections, the ultimate supremacy of the legislature, open criticism through freedom of speech, of the press, of assembly. Courts must be nonpolitical. The individual must be protected by the tested procedure of fair and speedy trials and by denial to the government of improper searches and seizures or the power to inflict cruel punishments, methods always resorted to by police states.

There is a trend now taking place in the world to express men's longing for greater security in terms of their legal right to that security. Emphasis is on "economic democracy," which, according to the Communists, is ignored in the "bourgeois" state. The Soviet constitution of 1936 guarantees "the right to work," "the right to rest and leisure," "the right to maintenance in old age and also in case of sickness or loss of capacity to work," "the right to education."[7] Full employment, according to their theory, becomes a duty of the state. The new Italian republic, brought into being by the constitution of December 22, 1947, recognizes the obligation to provide work for all its citizens. "The Republic," under Article 32, "protects health as a fundamental right of the individual and as an interest of society and guarantees free care to the indigent." By Article 36 "the worker has the right to a compensation proportionate to the quantity and quality of his labor and in any case sufficient to assure him and his family a free and dignified existence." The tendency in our country, which I have earlier noted, to substitute a more direct participation by the people in the activities of government is paralleled in Italy by a provision which permits the people to exercise "initiative in legislation by proposal of a bill . . . supported by at least 50,000 electors" and by the authorization of a referendum "to determine the abrogation, total or partial, of a law (within certain specified limitations)" when demanded by 500,000 electors. Yet "the republican form is not subject to constitutional amendment." Amendment of any of the other articles of the constitution might be held unconstitutional by the new

Italian Constitutional Court, which has powers similar to those of our Supreme Court, on the ground that the change violated the inalienable fiat establishing a republican form of government. Thus what is given to the people by way of promise of economic security may be at the price of the surrender of political freedom. And the ancient dilemma appears under a new form.[8]

The recognition of economic rights is further illustrated by the action of the United Nations Commission on Human Rights. The Commission, of which Mrs. Franklin D. Roosevelt, the United States member, is chairman, adopted on June 18, 1948, and sent to the Economic and Social Council of the United Nations an International Declaration of Human Rights, and the uncompleted draft of a covenant, to be completed at a later meeting. The declaration would require acceptance only by the Assembly, without further action by the member-nations, and would therefore be nothing more than the expression of a moral obligation, "a common standard of achievement for all peoples and all nations." The covenant, on the other hand, would be a treaty which would impose definite legal sanctions on the ratifying states.

We find, in the declaration, in addition to personal and political safeguards, a recognition of the economic rights which I have noted. "Everyone has the right to work, to just and favorable conditions of work and pay, and to protection against unemployment . . . to equal pay for equal work . . . to a standard of living, including food, clothing, housing and medical care, and to social services, adequate for the health and well-being of himself and his family, and to security in the event of unemployment, sickness, disability, old age or other lack of livelihood in circumstances beyond his control. . . . Mother and child have the right to special care and assistance. . . . Everyone has the right to education . . . to rest and leisure . . . to participate in the cultural life of the community."[9]

These articles in the declaration are a recognition of the growing belief that an obligation of the modern state is to insure against unemployment and personal economic disaster. They indicate that most men will insist on security as well as liberty—perhaps in preference to liberty. Whether such "rights," with corresponding public duties, should be expressed in an international statement is a different matter. The conservative, urging caution, will suggest that it is cruel to mislead "everyone, everywhere in the world" with promises of a perfection which cannot be fulfilled, certainly not now, probably never. But, answers the progressive, we approach realization only if the aspiration glows with the fire of a universal dream. The rights which we have written into our basic charter are not everywhere enjoyed by all Americans; but their expressed affirmation has led men nearer the goal and has spurred them to cherish these freedoms and to try to make them actual. No modern democratic government can long endure without acknowledging responsibility to its citizens for assuring them a decent physical and cultural life. The Atlantic Charter is a recognition of this responsibility.

Recently the Supreme Court of the United States granted certiorari and heard argument in three cases involving racial restrictive covenants. The trial courts, sustained on appeal, had enforced the restrictions so as to preclude Negroes from purchasing and occupying real estate, to prevent owners from selling or leasing their property to Negroes, and to eject Negroes from property they were occupying. The American Association for the United Nations filed a brief *amicus curiae*, in favor of the Negroes, basing its argument on the language of the United Nations Charter. Article 55 (c) provides that "the United Nations shall promote . . . uniform respect for and observance of, human rights and fundamental freedoms for all without distinction as to race, sex, language, and religion." In the following article members pledge themselves "to take joint and separate action . . . for the achievement of the purposes set forth in Article 55." The right to acquire and occupy property without discrimination—so the Association argued —was surely one of the "fundamental rights" thus protected. Enforcement of these racial restrictions, it was urged, was a violation of the covenants to which the United States was pledged by treaty, which became the supreme law of the land, invalidating any conflicting provisions of state common law or statutes, expressing a public policy which must guide the actions of American courts. The Supreme Court, without referring to the Charter, held that the covenants were unenforceable. I cite the argument, however, to show the importance that our new foreign policy of united democratic action with other countries may have on our underlying theories of rights and liberties. A discrimination which before could be overlooked in the refined distinctions of our settled racial prejudices might no longer flourish in the broader international field. Our announced sense of brotherhood with all the people in this new world, finding expression in the Charter, might now rise above our traditional intolerance.

If we seek to enlist those who waver between the choice of democracy and that promised by the religion of state worship, we must show them that we do live freely. Much is said for their consumption of the high standard of living which free enterprise has afforded Americans. It is harder to emphasize the high standard of individual liberties which free political institutions have achieved when they exist only for a part of our population.

Yet if many have held up our failures and inconsistencies, and discounted our preaching by our practices, the thought of America has also meant to countless men and women a renewed faith in living. Eight weeks after Pearl Harbor, immediately following a radio speech I had made about the registration of aliens, a young refugee girl who had recently come to this country wrote me from Radcliffe College: "I don't need to tell you that we—perhaps even more than you 'real' Americans—wandering, uprooted, and haunted, as we have been for the last eight years, need your United States: not just as a piece of land, a material living space; for much more than that. We need America to regain our faith in living, and dying; human beings, and, above all, young people, do not live on bread alone; we have the urge of being loyal to something on this earth, of pledging our allegiance to some Flag; we crave to be let to love, and be at least accepted in return. We want to know why we breathe, and eat, and study; why we should work, get married, and have children. We need America to give us an answer."

VII

DEMOCRACY, SOCIALISM, AND
FREE ENTERPRISE

*

I HAVE considered two of the underlying traits of the American outlook—distrust of government and a firm belief in the "natural" laws of competition and laissez faire, both normal accompaniments of individual self-reliance. I have noted that these conceptions, rising from a theory of democratic action to a moral dogma, have in practice been steadily yielding to the advance of the service state as the problems of society became more complex and that those who were loudest in denunciation of public enterprise were ready to accept government aid when it suited their particular interests.

I should like to explore in this chapter the habit of mind which first identifies democracy with free enterprise and then concludes that socialism, which is the opposite of a system based on private ownership, is for that reason opposed to the democratic point of view.

In Continental Europe the acceptance of a competitive society as the hypothesis of a free life never became as deeply intrenched in men's minds as with us. The nineteenth-century free trade had evolved from a feudalism which had never existed in the American colonies. The idea that government should be active in business affairs was not so alien to European thinking as to ours. State monopolies and barriers to internal trade of the seventeenth and eighteenth centuries were gradually discarded; but the tradition of government, inherited from one generation to another, was carried in the mold of respect rather than in the angle of distrust of authority which so greatly influenced the organization of our Constitution. Europe was not like America, where individualism came naturally to a new country unlimited by the inhibitions of the past or the resources of the future. "Unbridled capitalism," as our system appeared to many of the older nations, did not seem to them to be an economic law or moral necessity.

To many Americans insistence on a "free" capitalist society has in the past few years increased at the same time that its application was waning in practice. Instinctively conservative and comfortably prosperous, uninterested in and therefore blissfully ignorant of "foreign ideologies" and "alienisms," unshakeable in their assurance that the "American way of life" was the chief cause in producing a prosperity and standard of living higher than the world had ever experienced, they could see no reason why the simple rules which had guided their direction should not be applied to other countries. Take off the controls, get government out of business, let the law of supply and demand reassert itself. They watched the spreading acceptance of socialism outside the United States with acute discomfort, challenging what they most valued, threatening their "way of life," a phrase which applied more to their own material prosperity than to their interest in a broader enjoyment of individual liberties. Socialism to them was essentially a system under which the government owns, operates, and controls the entire economy, and all individual effort gives way to paternalism. Socialism soon becomes, in the frame of such an oversimplified definition, indistinguishable from communism. Both systems—so the argument runs—are totalitarian, the extreme opposite of democracy, political and economic ways of living that cannot exist in a democratic environment. The two isms are lumped together as the common foe of all free men (or at least free Americans). The issue thus put is uncomplicated by the vexing difficulties of knowledge or thought. There need be no refined distinctions of intellectuals and college professors who seek to confuse the average citizen. There it is. What kind of world do you want? Make your choice.

Thus the American politician, his conservative instincts shrinking from the havoc which the changing facts of history play with all static concepts, rediscovered, for 1948, the familiar issue, which should be stated in a simple form that anyone can understand. On November 17, 1947, in his call to reconvene the Congress, President Truman recommended an anti-inflation program. He requested power to regulate credit and the distribution of scarce commodities, to strengthen rent control, and to utilize rationing and price control on a selective basis. A few days later Representative Jesse P. Wolcott, of Michigan, chairman of the House Committee on Banking and Currency, announced that the President's program to stabilize the domestic economy was "as opposite to the American system as socialism is the opposite of democracy. . . . The battle between the ideological forces of socialism and the American way of life, based upon our Constitution, rages on. . . . Socialism versus Democracy, capitalism versus managed economy, regimentation versus free enterprise. These are the issues which must be met squarely . . . before we can ever hope for economic and social stability in America and peace through the world."[1] The statement is a fair illustration of the type of appeal to American folklore that I have been trying to suggest: democracy means free enterprise; free enterprise is the American way; that is written in the American Constitution; socialism is the opposite of democracy, so cannot be allowed to go on if we are to have prosperity and peace through the world. The President had urged that we use certain controls calculated to check the rising cost of almost all goods, which was swinging us around in the dizzy whirlwind of inflation. That it might be wise to think about stabilizing the domestic economy, particularly now that we were planning to supply such heavy foreign demands, would not seem to be intrinsically unrealistic, let alone totalitarian. Mr. Wolcott was, of course, fully aware when he used these words that rising prices create a pretty warm political issue, and the chances were that the issue would still be not only alive but far lustier a year hence. What to do about prices would certainly interest the practical mind of the American voter, perhaps even more than an appeal to sustain the American way of life—whatever that meant. He might answer: "Never mind the way of life; what are you going to do about the cost of living?" In this tangible dilemma that Mr. Wolcott should have instinctively turned to this venerable abstraction indicates how strongly he at least believed in its effectiveness. The issue, Mr. Wolcott told the Economic Club at the Hotel Astor in New York, had been laid "squarely before the American people." "But what issue?" the people might ask. Do you want any controls, and which? The economic situation was similar to a war economy—goods were scarce, labor short, large exports had to be made, prices were spiraling. If controls were all right in the war, why were they now suddenly un-American? Was not the question rather which controls would prove effective? If effective, should we hesitate to use them?

Let us examine Mr. Wolcott's assumptions a little further. Controls meant socialism; discarding controls, relying, that is, on the play of competitive forces, was "the American way of life based upon our Constitution." But it is by no means true to say that control of prices was opposed to the American system or accurate to suggest that resort to such controls was repugnant to the Constitution, particularly during an emergency, which this period admittedly was. "The Fourteenth

Amendment," Mr. Justice Holmes once remarked, "does not enact Mr. Herbert Spencer's *Social Statics*."[2] Years before the Declaration of Independence the Colonial legislatures, following the example that Parliament had been practicing for four centuries, fixed the prices of many commodities and services. Statutes of eight of the thirteen states adopted during the Revolution fixed the price of almost every commodity in the market. The states continued to fix prices long after the Revolution. As late as 1857 the constitutionality of a Louisiana law conferring on the city of New Orleans the power to fix the prices of meat and bread was sustained by the state supreme court, following a similar decision of the Alabama supreme court.[3] Rent control by the state of New York during the emergency that followed the first World War was held constitutional by the Supreme Court of the United States and was adopted by the Congress of which Mr. Wolcott was a member. Following the depression of 1929 the price of milk, under judicial approval in numerous test cases, was fixed by municipal regulation.

Immediately before Congress convened, Representative Joseph W. Martin, Jr., speaker of the House, told the National Association of Manufacturers that the President's demand for controls "could easily mark the end of our American system of free government, free economy and free society. It could start our slide into the abyss of the police state."[4]

Senator Taft's angry reaction to the President's proposals that they were "a step to a completely totalitarian nation"[5]—later, it is true, modified by the tacit admission that several were not unreasonable and hence not totalitarian and might be safely considered—nicely indicates the irrational vexation of the conservative temperament when the absolute theory will not fit the facts. Perhaps, he may have thought later, as he had a little more time to muse on this irritating dilemma, the word "totalitarian" may have been a little strong. Although preserving our freedom is more important than keeping down prices, the public might not think so. The *New York Times* commented: "But it is to be hoped we will be spared the anguished cries of those who raise the spectre of totalitarianism whenever a government attempts to combat an emergency with emergency measures."[6]

The controversy between Mr. Truman and his controls and Mr. Wolcott and his free enterprise is not without interest. On December 10 Mr. Wolcott introduced the Republican program in the form of a joint resolution. As spokesman for the House leadership, he said that "it was not thought advisable in peacetime to put into any individual's hand, whether he be the President or anybody else, the power to change our form of Government from a democracy to that of a socialistic state."[7] The bill extended export controls for a year and authorized regulation of the use of railroad equipment. The rest of the plan, the portion primarily dealing with high prices, authorized "voluntary accords" by allowing businessmen to reduce prices and by removing the imagined threat of antitrust action if they did so. The circular reasoning that preceded this legislative achievement must have been about as follows: Supply and demand fix prices. This natural law will bring prices down. If you try to curb the law, prices will go up, because the market, which insists on being open, will be chiefly black. Businessmen attempt, quite properly, to get the highest prices they can in the open market under the natural law. But businessmen are patriots and undoubtedly will act like patriots in this national crisis and get together to overcome the natural law and keep prices down. Five dollars more per ton for steel was the answer of the businessmen. The law was working all right.

The average little man on the street, as he again tightened his belt, must have been a bit more skeptical of these ultimates. The sacred law was driving costs up instead of down, and he is told only, for his thinning comfort, that the natural process would indefinitely continue. "The people cannot see, but they can feel."[8]

President Truman signed the bill, calling it pitifully inadequate and pointing out that, since he had requested the controls, six weeks before, butter in Washington had risen from eighty-eight cents a pound to $1.05; shoes in Pittsburgh from $8.72 to $9.38 a pair; and the price of hogs in Chicago from $24.75 to $26.40 a hundred pounds.

On the same day Congressman Charles A. Halleck, House majority leader, acclaimed the legislation as an affirmation of the "American voluntary way of life. . . . The American people . . . have faith and confidence in our historic American way—the way of competitive enterprise—the way that has produced the goods for which the whole world pleads, and which the President is so eager to give away for years to come." The new law was in marked contrast to the Administration's effort "to regiment the American people."[9]

Mr. Taft muttered a word or two about "police-state powers" and declared that the great issue in the election the following November would be "whether the American people desire to set up a totalitarian government, a state which will direct every detail in the lives of its citizens."[10]

Where, then, does this confused thinking lead?

Most immediately it found expression in suggestions, sometimes direct and explicit, sometimes implicit, that a condition to our extending assistance under the European Recovery Plan should be that the governments to whom the assistance was tendered turn away from socialism. Surprisingly, Harold Stassen, a candidate for the presidency, and, therefore, his ear tuned to what he considered the people would respond to, was of this view, not merely tossing off a hot generality in a campaign speech but coolly putting it all down in the irrevocable pages of a book, *Where I Stand;* Stassen, mind you, the prime internationalist of his party, who had waged war on the laggard isolationists, who had vigorously supported all moves for a tighter world, wanted our aid conditioned on agreement by the recipient countries of Europe to desist from nationalization programs. Socialism and communism, he announced, were as indistinguishable as "two peas from the same confining pod."[11] As Arthur M. Schlesinger, Jr., reviewing the book, drily observed: "What kind of sense does Mr. Stassen's position make? . . . If Britain refuses to accept aid conditioned upon her surrender of the power of self-government, are we then to deliver Western Europe to the U.S.S.R. and find solace in the thought that we have preserved our capitalist virginity?"[12]

Thomas Dewey, then Mr. Stassen's formidable rival, was quick to see the weakness of Mr. Stassen's position. In a speech backing United States aid for Europe, at a dinner of *Forbes Magazine* for fifty foremost business leaders, also significant because it was his first definite utterance on foreign policy, the governor of New York rejected the suggestion that we should not help any nation that had nationalized its industry. "So long as human liberty is maintained," he said, "as a principal objective of a government that government is our friend."[13]

Raymond Moley suggested that, so far as possible, loans be made to private industries, instead of to governments, regretfully admitting that it would be hardly possible to impose "non-nationalization conditions," hoping, however, that the "trend toward nationalization" could be halted by this simple device. This, he thought, would be the normal course to follow, since "*the objective of the Marshall Plan*" was "*to re-establish free* enterprise as a barrier to statism in all forms" (the italics are mine, but the sentiments Mr. Moley's).[14]

On November 10, 1947, Earl Bunting, president of the National Association of Manufacturers, announced a program for foreign aid which had been adopted by the board of directors. The first "condition" included in the program was that "the nations receiving economic aid from the United States should not undertake any further nationalization programs, or initiate projects which have the effect of destroying or impairing private competitive enterprise." On January 23, 1948, Curtis E. Calder, chairman of the board of Electric Bond and Share Company, on behalf of the Association, proposed the same condition to the Senate Foreign Relations Committee, saying: "Considerable experience with post-war economic aid by the United States to some other countries indicates that at times such countries put nationalization programs ahead of recovery, and that such experiments result in an equality of misery instead of incentives based on production."[15] The day before, Senator C. Wayland Brooks, of Illinois, had remarked that the money proposed to be advanced to Europe would be "dissipated the same way as the $3,750,000,000 given to Great Britain to help subsidize their socialistic governmental practices."[16] From such an important and influential source as the N.A.M. the suggestion, given wide publicity, was particularly harmful in connection not only with the plan for European recovery but with the broader implications of our foreign policy growing out of that plan. These implications involve a drawing-together of Great Britain, the countries of western Europe, and the United States for a closer economic and political co-operation. To suggest, on the eve of the birth of the new policy, that we did not like the economic systems of our new allies, that we believed that their governments were postponing recovery by playing politics, and that therefore their Socialist practices must be changed before the economic revival could begin was hardly calculated to make friends and keep them.

During the discussions of the European Recovery Plan it was argued, on one hand, that aid to Europe—i.e., Socialist

Europe—if successful, would help the present Socialist governments. Alternatively it was said that, as European economy
was re-established through our help, European nations would
tend to tread again the virtuous paths of a free economy. But
such considerations are irrelevant. The political evolution of
Europe will not and should not be thus influenced by our
economic help. What Europe needs is a few years of breathing
space. It needs to learn how to build and operate an economy
which is unified in a single great field of exchange, as the
American economy was unified after the Constitution broke
down the competitive sovereign activities of the thirteen
states. Today in Europe in the same manner nations separate
and divide what could be a single Continental market. They
must find a new unity and the new strength which that unity
will bring. But that does not mean that they need to submerge
their independence or abandon the political institutions which
they have freely adopted.

Much of the criticism of the European Recovery Plan was
based on the belief that no help should be extended to countries as long as they exercise controls thought of as natural to a
Socialist state. Let them throw off the controls, it was said, so
that they can get back to free competition that will open the
world markets to trade. More specifically the talk was leveled
at Great Britain. What is her present situation?

It is estimated that World War II drained Britain's wealth to
the extent of one-quarter of her total assets. Government cal-
culations indicate that she will have to export 75 per cent
more goods than before the war in order to balance her international payments. Exports, in spite of the terrific war destruction—four million houses, for instance, destroyed or dam-
aged—had by mid-1947 exceeded pre-war levels. The Labour
government inherited an economy plagued by unemployment
and underproduction supported on the dole, a system of publicly fostered monopolies, a balance-of-payments deficit in

foreign trade amounting in 1938 to seventy million pounds. Between the two wars, under a Conservative administration, the country devoted only 3 per cent of its national income to the creation of new capital. Economists estimate that from 10 to 15 per cent should be so used. Under the Labour government about 5 per cent has, until lately, been going into capital development. Before the war the owners of the coal mines and of other industries had failed to improve them with modern equipment, a failure which largely accounts for the plight of English industry today. "The National income, estimated at some £4.6 billion in 1938, is about twice that figure today [end of 1947]. . . . Consumer expenditures in 1946, according to the [Government] White Paper, about equaled those for 1938. . . . Britain's general level of production in 1947 was up 10 to 20 per cent above pre-war output." That record is not so bad for a country still bleeding from the terrible onslaught of the war. Weekly per capita consumption of meat in the United States in 1947 was 95 ounces, while rationing in England allowed every person 18 ounces. An American consumed about three and a half quarts of milk and eight eggs weekly. In Britain the allowance was one quart of milk and one egg.[17]

Under these conditions the suggestion that the "experiments" of government rationing, allocations, and other controls result in an equality of misery and that they should be discarded in favor of the "incentives" of free enterprise reaches a glib impertinence equaled only by its thoughtless stupidity. We insist, on the one hand, that the governments of western Europe plan their economy over a period of years, that they undertake to see that an agreed portion of the advances are used for the creation of capital goods, that they strictly police expenditures; and, on the other, we inveigh against attempts at public planning as "Socialist" experiments which will interfere with the incentives to work calculated to produce "normal" recovery.

Actually the British government is using both national planning and the techniques of private enterprise to revive her economy. Most of the controls are not expressions of Socialist planning but are the necessary measures adopted by a government bent on building the country's export trade and distributing as equitably as possible the segment of the total production allocated to domestic consumption. Typical is the allocation of raw materials to insure that they go into export industries. The controls are similar to those we used during the war. And England today is in the midst of a war for survival.

Fortunately for the Marshall Plan, its chief supporters took the view that political conditions should not be tacked to the legislation. The President's Committee on Foreign Aid, of which Secretary of Commerce Harriman was the chairman, recommended that, although the loans should depend on the recipients' taking practical steps to achieve production, "aid from this country should not be conditioned on the methods used to reach these goals, so long as they are consistent with basic democratic principles. Continued adherence to such principles is an essential condition to continued aid, but this condition should not require adherence to any form of economic organization or the abandonment of plans which call for a different form of economic organization if they have been adopted and carried out in a free and democratic way." Foreign aid should not be used as a means of requiring other countries to adopt the American system of free enterprise, which "would constitute an unwarranted interference with the internal affairs of friendly nations."[18]

Henry L. Stimson saw the issue clearly. Now that we have become "a wholly committed member of the world community," by no choice of our own but as a result of the force of circumstances, we must realize that action will have to be in the world as it is and not as we would wish to have it. "It is a world in which we are only one of many peoples and in which our basic principles of life are not shared by all our neighbors. . . . We are building world peace, not an American peace. Freedom demands tolerance, and many Americans have much to learn about the variety of forms which free societies may take. . . . We shall not be able to separate the sheep from the goats merely by asking whether they believe in our particular economic and political system. Our coöperation with the free men of Europe must be founded on the basic principles of human dignity, and not on any theory that their way to freedom must be exactly the same as ours. We cannot ask that Europe be rebuilt in the American image."[19]

The State Department was fully aware of the dangers inherent in political limitations attached to the European Recovery Plan. Apparently Secretary of State Marshall had this in mind when, in December, 1947, he said at the Pilgrims' Dinner in London that the difference between the Socialist economy of Great Britain and capitalism in the United States offers "no serious difficulties" to continued development of "close and even fraternal relationship" between the two countries. We must not let our fear of socialism adversely affect our relations to Socialist countries. If American democracy is identified with free enterprise, it will be thought of by most liberal Europeans as a doctrinaire and reactionary movement. Political conditions to European recovery will be resented everywhere in Europe as unwarranted attempts to dominate the life of European nations whose political integrity and freedom we are professing to save. The Soviet attack on the Marshall Plan continually reiterated that it was calculated to violate the sovereignty of European nations and to dictate to them a "reactionary" economic policy. The Communists will be quick to point to any such political limitations on the administration of the plan as evidence of American economic imperialism.

Such clear strictures on free national sovereignty have not found a place in the E.R.P. statute. Yet policy is not achieved or exhausted by its affirmation in formal law. It is constantly changed in the daily administration of the law out of which it rises. "The operation of this program [E.R.P.]," Secretary Marshall said, "will in many ways define and express the foreign policy of the U.S. in the eyes of the European countries and the world."[20]

Yet on May 12, 1948, Paul G. Hoffman, economic co-operation administrator, testified before the Senate Appropriations Committee that he would probably refuse to assist the United Kingdom to develop an industry which the British government had determined to nationalize. His discretion in making such a determination is doubtless authorized by the broad provisions of the act, which directs the governments sharing in its benefits to make "efficient and practical use" of their resources. "We would have to decide," said Mr. Hoffman, "whether socialization would make for recovery. My guess is that it would not." He explained that his action would be guided by economic and not political considerations. But, whatever motives impelled such a decision, it would be political and would be taken against the national policy of the government with which he was dealing.[21]

The original draft of the bilateral treaty with France to cover the operations of the interim program of American aid is reported to have contained a provision requiring the French government to agree that full publicity should constantly be given to the amount, extent, and form of that aid, including broadcasting over government stations.[22] Could it really have been seriously considered that such an advertisement of charity would have created a friendly and spontaneous gratitude on the part of the recipient? Even though a provision for publicity appeared in the Emergency Foreign-Aid statute, was it necessary to rub it in again in the supplementary treaty?

We should regard the European countries to whom aid is being extended as partners. If our role is conceived of in that relation, we shall be less likely to indulge in blunders or put forward restrictions to the help which will be galling to the other members of the partnership. We must realize, if the partnership is to succeed, how much tact and tolerance on our part are essential to make a go of it. The discussions of the Marshall Plan imagined a different relationship—that of creditor and debtor. And it is not unnatural that, only now half-awake to the immense responsibilities which have come to us—for we have not sought them—in this reshuffled world, we should still visualize our relation to Europe in the same terms that prevailed in the years that followed the first World War. If we are merely to lend or give money to a debtor, who did not pay his debts the last time, without security, what is the sense of it? Why waste all this money instead of applying it to reduce our own swollen taxes?

Such an attitude misses the point of the relation, the essential quality which should guide our new adventure in humanity. It is not only that Europeans are cold and hungry, unable to produce because their tools of production have been largely destroyed, and that ours have not. It is not charity— surely not charity. Nor is it only that European recovery is essential to our own ultimate well-being, and a wise business judgment indicates the desirability of our help. It is also that in those sixteen European nations today there are men who hold dear and will fight for the decent values of human dignity traditional to Western culture, out of which American civilization has grown splendid. To them we extend the help of our strong hand, just as we joined them—was it very long ago?— in a war against a similar threat to those values.

That we should not insist on trying to block socialization

programs is not in conflict with our advocating the reduction of national restrictions on foreign trade. Return to a greater measure of free trade is no more inconsistent with the nature of socialism than high tariffs are alien to free enterprise. Or, if an inconsistency exists, it is found in the imponderable realm of economic theory and not in the actual domain of national practice.

Suggestions such as those of Governor Stassen, Congressman Wolcott, and Mr. Moley show not only a profound ignorance of the nature of socialism, and of the difference between socialism and communism, but a complete misunderstanding of the conflicts which are shaking Europe today. In Continental Europe the political parties that are resisting the Communists are the Socialists. As the State Department told Congress, they are "among the strongest bulwarks in Europe against communism." It is they who stand between the two extremes of left and right, at one end the Communists, at the other what is left of the ultraconservative group—the monarchists, the landlords, and the dregs of the pre-war autocrats and Fascists, whom the people dread and hate. In a very actual sense these ultraconservatives, seeking to revive their old privileges and dominance, push the public toward the extreme left. In the French strikes in November, 1947, it was the French workmen, Socialists by long tradition and until three years ago preponderently Socialists in the Confédération National du Travail, who sustained the government and supported the wise policy and firm action of Schumann, the Socialist prime minister. After the strike Jouhaux, the outstanding Socialist labor leader of France, broke away from the Confédération, now Communist-controlled, to form a new organization, the Force Ouvrière, which would be free from Communist domination and would compete with communism for the support of labor, a support which in the ultimate analysis will determine the fate of France. De Gaulle and the Gaullists may talk anti-communism. But, as an effective movement, they cannot rally the French people to a middle-of-the-road policy, because their conservatism represents the type of anti-democratic absolutism to which the people will not willingly return, even if they have to fight a civil war to prevent it. The political stability of France today can be reached only in a continued and strengthened liberal government, centered around the Socialist movement, a government which the United States should back not only in the polite formulas of dignified diplomacy but to which Americans should look, with conviction and enthusiasm, as the chief hope for a moderate yet free system not only in France but in all western Europe. If that is realized, we shall be less likely to make the egregious blunder of sending a semiofficial diplomatic representative to learn from interviews with General de Gaulle the temper and condition of France—conferences which are, of course, given immense publicity and cause consternation among the "liberal" bloc, who wish to think of America as turned in the direction of democracy, and look upon De Gaulle as a symbol of reaction, although they once regarded him as a symbol of resistance.

The alternative to communism in Europe is not capitalism but some form of socialism. Europe will not return to free enterprise in the sense that most Americans attach to that phrase. We may like this situation or not, it may portend progress or stagnation, but it must be accepted as the hypothesis on which the greater part of European political thinking is based. Europeans will not go back to their old order.

But, it may be argued, does not the Conservative trend in the municipal elections in England show that the Conservatives are coming back to power before many years have elapsed? I will not venture to prophesy whether this election was an indication of a return to power of the Conservative party or merely a recorded resentment against the irritating controls and dreary hardships that voters have had to put up with. Such a keen observer as Anne O'Hare McCormick thought that the voters were "not voting against the limited nationalization measures Labor has put into effect . . . [but] against the conditions of life."[23] But I refer to "The Industrial Charter," a statement of Conservative policy adopted at a meeting of the party at Brighton in October, 1947. The charter, as was to be expected, paid its respect to "a system of free enterprise" and opposed "nationalization as a principle upon which all industries should be organized"; but it added: "We do not believe that it will be desirable to restore to private ownership the coal industry and the Bank of England." It did not suggest that railroads be returned to private hands. "Controls," said the charter, "breed like rabbits"; but it hastened to assure the public: "We will not remove the control from any necessity of life until we are certain that it is within reach of every family." And support of private enterprise did not prevent the British Conservatives from accepting the principle that "the Government must be responsible for maintaining a high and stable level of employment"; and that, to achieve this, it was "not enough to have, as some Socialists suggest, a programme of public works up the Government's sleeve" but that "in certain cases where there is a special and urgent need for capital equipment we shall be prepared to give special help through taxation."[24] Of course, all this does not add up to socialism. But neither does it add up to private enterprise, American brand. And this is the program of the party of Winston Churchill and Anthony Eden.

The leaders of the Soviet state know where the conflict divides in Europe. As to America, well—so apparently the argument runs—Marxians can afford to wait three or four years until the inevitable crash. But in Europe they know that the enemy of communism is socialism. There socialism is the choice of those men who still love liberty yet fear for their economic security. They wish to build a state that will secure them some economic assurance, yet leave them politically free. The selection is between the moderation of socialism and the savage extreme of communism. To the Soviet, therefore, European socialism must be crushed. The resolution adopted by the conference of Communists held in Poland in September, 1947, to revive the Comintern showed that plainly. "The Right-Wing Socialists," it declared, "are the traitors in this common cause . . . the Socialists in most . . . countries, and especially the French Socialists and the British Laborites—Ramadier, M. Blum, Mr. Attlee and Mr. Bevin—facilitate by their servile placidity the fulfillment of American capitalistic aims."[25]

VIII

SOCIALISM IS NOT COMMUNISM

☼

LET us take another look at the U.S.S.R. It must have been a difficult choice for the Russians to make when the generous sweep of Secretary Marshall's arrow in the air had raised the eyes of Europe to America and turned the faces even of her satellites toward this new source of help. How could she convincingly say to them, "You must not accept the promise of these good things, tainted with imperialist poison," and at the same time hold her control of their political leaders, caught between the true faith and hunger? After all, Communists have to eat too. Nationalism was by no means dead in the countries that were wavering. Their equivocal position became more difficult when Great Britain, France, and the United States offered to return Trieste to Italy. Trieste had been hard for the Italian Communists to swallow. The Soviet conviction must have been clearly held that the collapse in America could be counted on at a not too distant date, for the decision involved enormous risks. Light is thrown on the reasons for the decision in a very interesting conversation which Walter Lippmann reports that he had with a leading Communist of eastern Europe.[1] The Communist admitted that Europe and Russia would not recover without substantial help from the United States. "Then why do you prevent it?" The answer was that the United States would necessarily have to give the help after the great crash when she had fifteen million unemployed and must subsidize exports to keep her factories going. Then there would be no political strings tied to the help. Now there would be. In discussing the Marshall Plan, the Communist said that any help would "carry with it the condition—and here he cited Mr. Stassen—that Europe must give up Socialism. . . . 'You will,' he said, speaking with mounting enthusiasm, 'become more and more unpopular with the masses of Europe. . . . They will see that your dollars are being used to destroy their independence by stopping the socialism that they want.' " He obviously realized how useful from the Soviet point of view our dislike of socialism might become.

It is worth examining some of the basic differences between communism and socialism. I do not propose to get into the arid dialectics that separate the Marxists, the shade of party shift or drift, the denunciations and intricate subtleties which so delight the different brands of American Socialists and Communists. My point is much simpler. I believe that to determine the differences neither system can be adequately described solely in terms of economic and political theory but must also be considered in its ethical and human content. And theory should be tested by practice. We have before us a quarter of a century of the practice of Russian communism and, by contrast, in England a few brief years of accepted socialism. I do not suppose that the shorter experiment is sufficient to warrant altogether adequate comparison. But both experiments indicate the direction and the drift and serve to define the differences of these two ideologies as regards the position of the state in modern society. They show a basic divergence in theory as well as in practice.

The U.S.S.R. today practices socialism in one thing only—its ownership and operation of all basic industry, which is, of course, a Socialist *sine qua non*. In other respects it no longer resembles a Socialist state. "Socialism" is a vague word, its meaning and the extent of its application varying greatly in the different Socialist parties throughout Europe, whose very names imply their difficulties in agreeing on any universal theory or even general program. I do not refer to the Socialists of the extreme left, like Nenni in Italy, who vote the Communist party line, and who are, in fact, Communists retaining the Socialist sheep's clothing for practical activities of the wolf, missionary considerations useful for boring from within. Avowed Communists never refer to themselves as Socialists. The Soviet Union and its circle of satellites are "democracies," as we have so often heard Mr. Molotov reiterate, and all who are opposed to them are "Fascists." Soviet political science knows no shades but white and black, and all propaganda is reduced to the alternative of the simplest moral choice. During the trial at Nuremberg the Russian prosecutor and his assistants had many epithets with which to describe the German defendants. But they were always linked with "Fascist"— "Fascist dogs," "Fascist murderers," "Fascist assassins"— never "Nazi." The contrast had to be sharp and simple. "Fascist" was a word which could be used then and thereafter to apply to all enemies of the true faith, whereas "Nazi" had a provincial German sound and was not nearly inclusive enough.

We can disregard such semantic nonsense. Of course, communism is not democracy. It is almost as equally absurd to call it socialism. "The Leftist contention that Soviet economy (i.e., nationalization) *is* socialism is as spurious as the Rightist contention that state-controls and planning *are* Fascism."[2] Any honest Socialist will tell you—and document himself with endless references—that today the principles that guide the Soviet state are almost all opposed to Socialist ideology. "Most moderate Socialists," writes William Henry Chamberlin in one of his recent studies of Russia, "repudiate the idea of dictatorship altogether. They take the position that there cannot be genuine socialism without democracy, without freedom of election and trade-union organization, without respect for civil and personal liberties. Measured by these standards the Soviet Union cannot be called socialist."[3]

The belief in civil liberties and their protection by the kind of institutions which Western culture has gradually adopted is basic to European socialism, which implies none of the suppression of human liberties common alike to the Fascist, Nazi, and Communist state and is a very part of their avowed policy as well as their actual practice. The "bourgeois" ideals of a free press, open criticism, and nonpolitical courts are derided by totalitarian philosophers as out of date. How, indeed, can the state be supreme if they are permitted to exist? That supremacy is the cornerstone of the totalitarian philosophy which can be kept secure only by the use of the secret police. The totalitarian state—Italian, German, or Russian—is always founded on a political police, since the end and the aim are the suppression of criticism of the state, for man normally is a critical, dissenting, and garrulous creature. The ideal of socialism, on the contrary, is based on individual freedom; its goal is neither anti-democratic nor anti-Christian.

Examples of the difference in practice between the Socialist and Communist state are clearly outlined for us to see at this moment in the sharpness of their contrast. On the one hand stands Great Britain, a Socialist state, created by the deliberate and peaceful vote of her citizens; a system gradually evolved and still affecting a comparatively small segment of industry; her press free, her courts open, her elections effective (as shown in the Conservative drift in the municipal elections in November, 1947), and Mr. Churchill magnificently vituperative in a House of Commons controlled by an enormous majority of his opponents. The Labour government in Britain is attempting "to guarantee economic security within a framework of parliamentary democracy."[4] On the other hand is the

U.S.S.R., in which all freedoms are suppressed, the state supreme, criticism nonexistent, the courts political tools of the government, enemies of the state liquidated or penned in labor camps. These are the essentials of a totalitarian system.

Controls, in spite of President Truman's impulsive remark, are not those methods of the police state which distinguish it from the democratic state, for the police state does not permit controls freely chosen by the people to enforce a self-determined discipline. In the possibility of that choice lies the essential difference.

Of the basic rights I have mentioned in a previous chapter, all would be rejected by a totalitarian political realist, irrespective of whether he were Fascist or Soviet. And the reason is obvious. If the state is all-important, the individual nothing, criticism of the state is evil. It creates disunity and the waste of conflicting effort. It will, of course, not be permitted. From the same conception of complete, unchallenged sovereignty flows the part which each branch of the government must play. With us the court is outside the government, independent of it, standing between citizen and sovereign. In the totalitarian state the court is but an arm of the sovereign, organized to carry out his will, never placed in a position to oppose him. Thus, when Hitler was creating the Nazi state, the power of the courts had to be broken before his domination was established. If political judgments are to be the result of fiat and not of the give-and-take of compromise, they cannot be questioned once they have been promulgated. An essential element of the totalitarian state is that the courts, although sometimes preserving the appearance of judicial bodies to create the fiction of continuity with a more liberal past, must always carry out the political policies and decisions of the government. Political courts are a normal part of the police state. The International Military Tribunal at Nuremberg thus describes the integration of the courts into the Nazi system:

"Similarly, the Judiciary was subjected to control. Judges were removed from the Bench for political or racial reasons. They were spied upon and made subject to the strongest pressure to join the Nazi Party as an alternative to being dismissed. When the Supreme Court acquitted three of the four defendants charged with complicity in the Reichstag fire, its jurisdiction in cases of treason was thereafter taken away and given to a newly established 'People's Court,' consisting of two Judges and five officials of the Party. Special courts were set up to try political crimes and only party members were appointed as Judges. . . . Pardons were granted to members of the Party who had been sentenced. . . . 'Judges' letters' were sent to all German Judges by the Government, instructing them as to the 'general lines' that they must follow."[5]

Joseph Goebbels on March 17, 1942, notes in his diary that he is considering the suggestion whether he "ought not to send Party comrades as observers into the various courts so that they may quietly inform me and enable me to take measures against verdicts that do not correspond to the times." Three days later he records that he has "proposed a law to the effect that whoever violates the commonly known principles of National Socialistic leadership is to be punished with imprisonment and in very serious cases even with death. . . . *Justice must not become the mistress of the state, but must be the servant of state policy.*"[6]

Certain individual rights are supported by the U.S.S.R. constitution of 1936, but the provisions seem to be little more than formulas for fair procedure, limited in scope and always subject to the will of the state. The fiction of free elections is sustained. Article 134 of the constitution provides for elections "by the voters on the basis of universal, equal and direct suffrage by secret ballot." Joseph Stalin on December 22, 1947, received all 1,617 votes registered in his district in the

Moscow City Soviet election and 505 "complimentary" votes outside the city, presumably cast under the protection of this provision.[7] The fiction of a free press and freedom of speech and assembly is found in Article 125, which seeks to "guarantee" these rights "by placing at the disposal of the toilers and their organizations printing presses, supplies of paper, public buildings, the streets, means of communication and other material requisites for the exercise of these rights." Trials are held in public—"unless otherwise provided for by law." Arrests must be under court order or with the sanction of the state attorney; there is the "right of defense," provision for interpreters. But the N.K.V.D. (successor to the Cheka and the O.G.P.U.) may, for a crime deemed "socially dangerous," under the statutes of July 10, 1934, "impose, in a nonjudicial procedure, the penalty of imprisonment in a convict labor camp up to five years, exile with settlement in a certain locality for a period up to five years, and banishment."[8]

In the U.S.S.R. the state can do no wrong. This concept was well illustrated by the construction placed by the Soviet prosecutor on a clause of the Charter under which the international trial of the major German war criminals was held at Nuremberg. He had presented the report of a U.S.S.R. government commission tending to show that Polish officers had been killed in the Katyn Woods by Germans. A defendant petitioned the Tribunal to be permitted to produce witnesses to disprove this charge and to show that the Russians, and not the Germans, had done the killing. The Charter provided that the Tribunal might take judicial notice of government reports. This it had done. But the provision in the Charter must mean—so ran the Russian argument—that no other evidence could be listened to. Once a government had spoken, that was the final truth; how could it be disproved? The Tribunal ruled otherwise.

Any suggestion that an individual has rights above the

state, that he may challenge or resist state action, becomes treason in a highly developed totalitarian system. At a meeting of the Rumanian Lawyers Association on October 9, 1947, it was "made perfectly clear that no Rumanian attorney eager to succeed would want to defend Dr. Juliu Maniu and other Peasant party leaders." Members of the bar were forbidden to represent alleged violators of the monetary stabilization law. A National Peasant party lawyer, Emanoil Socor, protested that this infringed the fundamental right of any accused person to be represented by counsel if the trial was to be fair. He was howled down. A government supporter suggested that "it would be equally valid to contend that doctors should encourage epidemics to increase the number of their patients and that engineers should encourage earthquakes so that there would be more reconstruction activities."[9] Under the Communist conception a "right" can never arise where disobedience to the state is alleged to have occurred.

Two fundamental Socialist canons are equal opportunity for education and for employment and continued emphasis on improved economic and social environment as a means to individual development. Emphasis is on self-discipline rather than on rigid external state restraints on human beings, outside the essential realm of state industrial activity. Socialists believe that, if the economic environment is altered, a change in human nature will come from within and that it cannot be imposed from without. Proponents of the capitalist state differ from Socialists not on the desirability of equal opportunity but as to the extent that it can be furthered by public action and would, depending on whether they were conservative or radical, narrow or enlarge the existing pattern of that action. They hold that state activity in the industrial and commercial field is calculated less to free the spirit by controlling the environment than to kill the incentives which feed human vitality and originality.

Geoffrey Crowther, the editor of the London *Economist*, believes that from the point of view of their economic systems Russia and the United States resemble each other more "than either one resembles the structure of socialist idealism." He is of the opinion that the whole Soviet system has for a long while been out of character with socialism, evidenced most recently by Stalin's currency decree under which overnight a large percentage of the people's savings was wiped out by an action more like "the good old capitalist practice of insisting on sound money" than any expression of Socialist theory, which has always opposed policies of deflation as injurious to labor. Socialism may still be a religion, but it is no longer a practice in Russia today, except in the application of a single Socialist dogma—that all means of production must belong to the state. That the basic Socialist theory that the workman should get full value for his labor has been thrown overboard is indicated by the various five-year plans which, according to Mr. Crowther, "represent the biggest exploitation of the workers that ever existed." The consumer share of total production in Russia is less than in other countries, the share that goes into capital equipment greater. In Socialist states, on the other hand, "the rate of accumulation of capital has of late been alarmingly low." Mr. Crowther believes that there is nowhere else in the world such a thoroughgoing and deliberate system of monetary rewards and a greater inequality of earned incomes as in Russia.[10] Chamberlin had already remarked that the "Communist Party is taking on more and more the functions and psychology of a combination Rotary Club and National Association of Manufacturers."[11]

There is today cumulative evidence that whatever goes on in that dark country is not the practice of socialism. Nor, in

any exact sense, is it communism. It is the theory and practice
of totalitarian power by a comparatively small, deeply intrenched government bureaucracy. It is, of course, difficult to
obtain detailed information, particularly facts indicating to
what extent the operation of the Soviet state follows its
orthodox economic religion. Russian production has shown,
many economists believe, striking improvement. Yet they
warn us that Soviet statistics must be taken with great caution.[12] However, there is enough known of Russian laws,
decrees, and pronouncements to warrant the conclusion
reached by Mr. Crowther that the U.S.S.R. has abandoned
socialism.

According to Arthur Koestler and Chamberlin, Russia is
moving not toward but away from socialism. The Socialist
goal has often been expressed in the words: "From each according to his ability; to each according to his needs." This is
no longer a Communist doctrine. In the U.S.S.R. inheritance
was abolished after the Russian Revolution, in order to give
each child, according to the accepted Socialist dogma, an
equal opportunity at the start. In 1934 Stalin, addressing the
Seventeenth Congress of the Communist party, said: "To conclude that socialism demands equality and levelling of members of society . . . this is to talk rubbish and to slander
Marxism."[13] The "inequality" was reinstated by the constitution of 1936. Equality of educational opportunity was dropped
after 1932, so that today "on the average the children
of manual workers and peasants remain manual workers and
peasants, whereas the children of the upper strata are automatically put on the road to jobs in the upper strata."[14]
Chamberlin says that "scholarships are granted not to the
neediest, but to the most capable students." In 1938, 47.3 per
cent of the students were the children of government employees and "intellectuals." Free higher education was abolished in 1940.[15] The result, a deliberate government policy, is

that an "hereditary bureaucracy, technocracy and military caste emerges in the framework of a new type of class-society, based no longer on the ownership of the means of production, but on control of the levers of the state, and following the same trend towards self-perpetuation which characterizes all stable class rule in history."[16] David J. Dallin believes that this new "intelligentsia," a term which he says is almost identical with "government employees," constitutes the highest class of Russian society, comprising, at the beginning of World War II, ten to eleven million people, about 12 or 14 per cent of the active population. He calculates that this class received from 31 to 35 per cent of the national income in terms of "products distributed and not retained for the State's needs" and that the workers, who number a quarter of the population, receive about the same share. This can be taken, perhaps, to illustrate Stalin's definition of communism, in 1935, quoted by Mr. Dallin, when the idea of inequality was being incorporated into Communist ideology: "Communism means that in a Communist society everyone works according to his abilities and receives consumer goods not in accordance with what he produces but in accordance with his *needs as a culturally developed human being.*"[17]

The material gathered under the direction of Representative Everett M. Dirksen by the Legislative Reference Service of the Library of Congress in 1946 supports the conclusion that "since the rise of Stalinism we have had the spectacle of a Communist society where the greatest emphasis is being placed on inequality of treatment and reward as a spur to ambition and responsibility. . . . The difference between the scales in the Soviet Union and the United States is one of degree and trend—the Soviet Union maintaining wider differentials and showing a definite tendency to increase differentials and inequalities." In June, 1931, Stalin, in a speech at a meeting of factory workers, said: "It is necessary to organize such a system of wage scales as will take into account the difference between qualified labor and unqualified labor." Thereafter equalitarianism became "petty bourgeois," "counter revolutionary," and "rotten liberalism."[18]

The wide divergence in incomes Koestler illustrates by a comparison of army pay in different countries, a point also made by Crowther. It is not surprising that inequalities in the military caste of the U.S.S.R. should prove even more extreme than among the workers. In 1943 a private received 10 rubles a month, a colonel 2,400. In the British army a subaltern is paid four times as much as a private; in the Soviet army, one hundred times as much.[19]

Similar extremes are found in industrial wages. Sir Walter Citrine, general secretary of the British Trades Union Congress, reports the salary of the technical director of a shoe factory in Leningrad in 1935 at 2,000 rubles a month; the head of the children's boot department, 1,900 rubles; the head of the cutting department, 1,600 rubles; while the production workers averaged 125–250 rubles monthly. In the Kirov Engineering Works, employing thirty thousand workers, the chief construction engineer and the chief draftsman were each paid 1,800 rubles a month, while the workers earned between 120 and 475 rubles. At the Koganovitch Ball Bearing Works in Moscow the director and the chief engineer earned 2,000 rubles monthly; the wages of the workers were 106–496 rubles. Managers of coal mines in 1933 were paid 550–1,500 rubles a month, while manual workers averaged 133 rubles.[20] According to a Moscow paper (1936), sixty employees of a Donetz mine earned monthly wages of 1,000–2,500 rubles; seventy-five averaged 800–1,000 rubles; four hundred earned 500–800 rubles, and the remaining one thousand averaged 125 rubles.[21] Kravchenko reports that in 1938, when unskilled workers were earning 150 rubles, his monthly salary was 3,000 rubles. It is not without significance that 75 per cent of the total number of workers employed were, according to a Russian publication, being paid in 1938 on a piece-work basis.[22]

Mr. Chamberlin believes that the manual worker is losing his elected place in the economy. There are "substantial and growing differences in wages, salaries and standards of living." A factory manager or engineer earns much more than a skilled worker, who in turn gets two or three times as much as an unskilled worker. A university professor's salary runs from 1,100 to 1,500 rubles a month; an elementary-school teacher, from 270 to 400 rubles. A post-office director will get 1,200–1,800 rubles a month; a telephone operator, 190–320 rubles. Industrial workers in 1935 averaged about 213 rubles a month; office workers, 319 rubles; machinists, 540 rubles; engineers, 1,744 rubles; and lower-grade unskilled workers, 89 rubles. The use of liberal bonuses and differentials is increasing.[23]

The Russian government is not the government of the laboring class. Labor unions, the backbone of any Socialist regime, as they have proved to be in Great Britain, are no longer elected by the workers, who are not in practice permitted to strike, and there have been no strikes since 1921. The unions do not represent labor in fixing wages, which is left to the heads of industry. Integrated into the state bureaucracy, their task is "no longer to protect the interests of the workers but to strengthen labour discipline and promote maximum efficiency," under labor legislation permitting foremen to discharge without notice for "unsatisfactory output," which entails loss of the ration card and the right to dwelling space. N. M. Shvernik, president of the All-Union Central Council of Trade Unions, stated to the Council in April, 1941, that "the most important task facing the trade unions . . . was to concentrate the efforts of the workers on fulfilling the state plan of production for 1941"—in other words, speed-up.[24]

The pattern is familiar to the development of the police state. As early as April, 1933, Adolf Hitler ordered Roberty Ley, who was then the staff director of the N.S.D.A.P. (Nazi party), "to take over the trade unions," a direction so efficiently carried out by the S.A. and S.S., which brought into "protective custody" the union leaders, that by May 3 the party press service was able to announce that the Christian trade-unions, the last to be liquidated, had "unconditionally subordinated themselves to the leadership of Adolf Hitler." In the place of the unions the Nazi state set up the Deutsche Arbeits Front, controlled by the Nazi party, which all German workers were in practice forced to join.[25]

Destruction of individual liberties touches every aspect of life in the police state. Divorce in Russia is, in substance, made impossible. Passports are necessary for Russian citizens to travel within their own country. Illegal attempts to leave are punishable by death. Collective responsibility for crimes is fixed on the family. Capital punishment is applicable to twelve-year-old children. Coercion and intimidation within the iron walls "where dissent is officially identified with crime" replace the Socialist's emphasis on self-imposed disciplines.[26]

Nikola Petkov, the leader of the Agrarian party in Bulgaria, was executed in September, 1947, for his opposition to the Communist government. The nine Social Democrats, forming what was left of the Opposition, ventured four months later to criticize the budget. Premier Georgi Dimitrov, the Communist dictator of Bulgaria, warned them to remember the fate of Petkov and the Agrarians. "They broke their heads," he said, "and their leader is under the ground. Think this over."[27]

There are those who, during the late war, noting one of the changes to which I have referred—the steadily increasing gap of wages between the few at the top and the many at the bottom—comforted themselves with the pleasing reflection that Russia was, after all, turning back to free enterprise as she experienced the necessity of economic incentives to create and distribute goods. But if she appreciated these incentives, and modified her system accordingly, she never altered her complete state ownership of the means of production and distribution or permitted the profit system or any semblance of competitive freedom to regulate her economy. Her political structure resembled far more the corporate state of Mussolini and the Nazi dictatorship than the Socialist government of England or the capitalist democracy of the United States, which shared in common a traditional belief in the importance of individual liberties. The police state is neither socialism nor capitalism. The ultimate test of any system is for whom and for what ends the machinery of government is used. Russia is less concerned with the future welfare of her workers than with the present condition of her well-intrenched bureaucracy. Stalin, on March 3, 1937, talking to the party—there is but one—defined the core of this bureaucracy, the party, in terms of its semimilitaristic organization: three or four thousand leading executives, the generals; thirty or forty thousand middle executives, the party officers; and one hundred to one hundred and fifty thousand members of the Junior Party Commanding Staff, the N.C.O's.[28]

I have pointed to the changes in the Soviet ideology and practice since the October Revolution which show the distance that the Soviets have traveled away from socialism. They do not seem to affect, however, the attitude of the confused "liberal," who, following the Communist path with open heart but closed mind, refuses to notice any difference and continues to believe that the Soviets have created a true Socialist state, dedicated to the betterment of the human race.

He dismisses as "exaggerations" the information which be-
gins to accumulate about the slave-labor concentration camps
back of the curtain. He is shown the estimates; 6,000,000 in
the camps, according to Eugene Lyons, in 1933; 10,000,000
according to Siliga, in 1937, although Boris Souvarine puts the
figure at 15,000,000 for that year; 12,000,000 according to
Barmine in 1938; 10,000,000 according to Dallin in 1940;
18,000,000 according to Kravchenko in 1941; 17,000,000 according to Koestler in 1943; 14,000,000 according to White in
1945.[29] As evidence of such practices becomes too impressive to
dismiss as idle rumors, the "liberal" excuses them on the
ground that they are but excrescences on the system which will
eventually disappear. The end, for a time, at least, he reluctantly admits, may, after all, justify the means. It does not.
The end meets the ruthlessness of the means. The end cannot,
when the police state is achieved, be differentiated from the
means. The political police in Russia operates on the theory
that "it is better to make ten innocent persons suffer than to
let one counter revolutionary escape."[30]

The "liberal" who remains an addict to the dissolving drug
of communism clings earnestly to his illusions, insisting that
socialism and communism are indistinguishable, and meeting
the "free-enterpriser" on common ground.

A sample of this brand of rationalization appeared in an
editorial of the *New Republic*, of which Michael Straight was
the editor, and Henry A. Wallace the contributing editor, on
December 29, 1947. Mr. Straight leveled his criticism of the
European Recovery Program by complaining, among other
things, that it involved the attempt "to use the Socialists of
Europe against the Communists . . . an old State Department
game. In embracing them, the State Department strangles
them. . . . When we bind Europe's Socialists to us we isolate
them from their own peoples." What a queer conclusion for a
liberal to reach! Perhaps, as the *New Yorker* says, the liberal

"never feels he knows where the truth lies, but is full of rich memories of places he has glimpsed it in."[31] The substance of Mr. Straight's argument is that one must not support Socialists and resist Communists, because they are both moving in the same direction of liberalism and social reform; that they are really indistinguishable and to try to distinguish them and choose one rather than supporting both separates the Socialists from the Communists, "their own people," and strangles the Socialists by the noose of our reactionary help. Help to anyone, according to this pleasing doctrine, is forbidden unless also extended to the Communists, in equal parts I should assume. Mr. Straight appears to be an addict. To him socialism and communism are the same thing. Arm in arm with Mr. Wallace, he meets Congressman Wolcott and Raymond Moley, traveling on a different road, but finally standing in front of the same closed door.

To my argument that socialism and communism are distinguishable if you look closely at both of them, an unconvinced listener might take a position which cannot be casually dismissed. Granted, he would retort, that the ideals of socialism have been, certainly by now, thrown overboard by the Communists and that the Soviet state is nothing but an intrenched group of privileged rulers manipulating the power levers of government, nevertheless a comparison between the nascent and timid experimental socialism of England, hardly scrubbed behind the ears, cannot be made with the U.S.S.R., now ripe and mature in its full experience. The Soviet experiment, he would continue, indeed proves the point—that socialism must grow into the police state; that power is always self-increasing, like a snowball; that to control anything, industrially speaking, you must control everything, as our own recent attempt—any attempt—to fix prices has so adequately demonstrated. The Founding Fathers knew this, he would conclude, and were aware of the history of feudalism which rested on state monopolies as well as on autocratic political controls, the two sides of the same coin, and from that teaching were led to insert in our constitutional system the brakes on government activity which are generally construed to prevent undue interference by the government in the economic field.

The argument is not unimpressive. That clearheaded analyst of economic and political conditions, Walter Lippmann, developed it ten years ago in great detail in *The Good Society*. The choice between security and liberty is intolerable, he believes, but not inexorable. The design of the future, a society planned for the broad enjoyment of abundance, is not possible, for a directed society becomes "bellicose and poor." He finds similar faults in the gradual collectivism of Great Britain and of the United States, although they have shown no disposition to establish a military totalitarianism as in the more extreme forms of collectivism. He believes that the true function of government, the liberal doctrine of the early nineteenth century before it was debauched by the absurd extremes of laissez faire, is that of a judge under common law, rather than the conception to which I have referred as that of the service state—a conception which, he argues, must logically result in ever increasing the power of the state, until it becomes collectivist. "All collectivism, whether it be communist or fascist, is military in method, in purpose, in spirit, and can be nothing else."[32]

Henry Hazlitt in a compact little book, *Will Dollars Save the World?*, expressing the same point of view, has made the most effective attack on the European Recovery Plan that I have yet seen. He believes that not the destruction and dislocation of war but government policies of exchange controls, price controls, and trade barriers are chiefly responsible for the present economic crisis in Europe and that further loans, while those policies continue, will not alleviate but will tend to increase the present industrial plight. Socialism, he thinks, is at the root of the trouble. It "cannot permit economic liberty, and therefore in fact it must ultimately cease to permit any other important kind of liberty. . . . The history of the spread of socialism is in fact a history of the disappearance of peace, representative institutions, limited government, and personal liberty."[33] He does not document this sweeping generalization or suggest how it could be applied to England or to some of the Scandinavian countries, whose admirably balanced economies have been achieved under labor governments. Nor does he touch on the most difficult problem in capitalist societies, that of curbing the domination of private monopoly and the development of cartels which are increasingly making that society less competitive, without resort to the very methods of state controls which he so dislikes. On July 25, 1948, the Federal Trade Commission, in a report to the Congress, declared: "No stretch of the imagination is required to foresee that if nothing is done to check the growth in concentration, either the giant corporations will ultimately take over the country, or the Government will be impelled to step in and impose some form of direct regulation in the public interest."[34]

That state controls may be highly undesirable in some fields of economy does not prove that they should not be resorted to in others. Such discussions of general economic philosophies are likely to be arid, and one is forced into the narrower corner of kind and degree. I do not know what way along or between these patterns the future of our world will lie. But this argument is based on imperfect and limited experience, applicable in but a restricted sense to our own times. Perhaps I would be less tempted to weigh its warnings were I not personally a believer in the proved advantages in recent times to a substantial segment of the world of the workings of a limited competitive economic system. But that is not the whole world, and the future is never foreclosed by the past. Most of us accept the increasing controls largely because they appear to be necessary to give the competitive system a chance to operate with relative freedom. It is not a clear choice of state controls versus no controls but of the dominion exercised by the monopoly powers which have emerged from a system of free enterprise and the planned supervision of community action thought to be based on less prejudiced considerations. In practice, as I have earlier suggested, we have accepted more and more increasing state action in attempting to solve particular practical problems. Questions of degree—how far should you go—can never be solved by invoking generalities.

Socialism believes that man is capable of controlling his environment and preserving his liberties at the same time. Disagreement with laissez faire capitalism exists as to whether he is able to control his environment but not that he must preserve his liberties. If he cannot preserve them, nothing else matters.

Experience molds institutions, not the application of economic abstractions. Some unity within the scope of the social sciences is needed to balance and direct the terrible unity of the physical sciences. We cannot dismiss, as undemocratic, efforts by Socialist governments to find that unity in community undertakings even if they are not such as we would choose for ourselves.

Western Europe may not continue to accept socialism, but it is very clear that it will not return to the type of private capitalism which we admire. If we insist on that return, it will stand sullenly against us; if we reiterate it as the ultimate American glory, Europe will regard us as hopelessly conservative, our only object being to maintain our own economic supremacy, a supremacy which but underscores its helplessness. It will not react with enthusiasm to the beauty of free competition where competition against such a power as ours appears impossible. What chance under present conditions, it will ask, have its automobiles and moving pictures, the fruit of its worn-out textile machinery, its skill and labor against American mass production backed by American resources. And it will turn again to the narrowing circle of the old international discriminations. Those who advocate preaching American achievements to advertise the values of free enterprise will be disappointed in the results. Europe, outside the darkness of the Soviet Union, largely knows the results. If the emphasis were less on material than on human values, more on a qualitative than on a quantitative approach; if we spoke, when we speak, of our deep concern with the social and economic injustices that still prevail, injustices that we ourselves among our own people have but haltingly remedied; if we could stretch their imaginations—and our own—to believe that the ancient dream of a decent and peaceful yet free life may be achieved; and, finally, if Europeans felt that we were asking them, as men of good will, to help us realize mankind's unshakeable vistas, the frustrations that oppress men's souls might yield before a moral positiveness which accompanied a material program. For the struggle today is over the soul of Europe.

Every nation of western Europe is today afraid that its nationalism will be absorbed in the insatiable imperialism of Soviet Russia. This imperialism in the past has fed on a false preaching of the international solidarity of labor and of the Socialist parties of the world. It is false politically, because the unity is not international but Russian, and false morally, because the love of a man's native land carries a necessary responsibility for the liberties he associates with what is his own. Therefore we must respect the free nationalism which western Europeans still cherish. I do not mean the chauvinism which preaches national supremacy—my nation right or wrong—and thrusts toward a place in the sun. I have in mind the decent love of hearth and home, the human links of inherited customs and memories of an accumulating past, the pride in one's own culture, to which these desperate people are reaching back for, now that so much of it has been destroyed. Out of the decay of this nationalism sprang the treachery of William Joyce and of John Amery, of Ezra Pound and of the Canadian citizens who betrayed the secrets of their government because they thought that secret information should be internationally shared. As Rebecca West has so poignantly written: "They needed a nation which was also a hearth. It was sad to see them, chilled to the bones of their souls, because the intellectual leaders of their time had professed a philosophy which was scarcely more than a lapse of memory, and had forgotten, among much else, that a hearth gives out warmth."[35]

IX

THE AMERICAN GOVERNMENT IN
THE NEW WORLD

✻

THE sense of urgency, of tragic events occurring before we can do anything to prevent them, of an irrational and irresponsible world, has hovered in the background of our consciousness since the mad split between the East and the West. The absorption of Czechoslovakia by Russia jarred us into a realization of the terrible speed with which history was being shaped, and there was a rush to build up our armed strength overnight, as if the enemy were on our border and we had not a day to lose. When we reflect on its habitual deliberative caution, it is curious with what speed Congress can move when some wave of mass fear or hysteria trembles through its ranks. The Senate took three months to confirm Lilienthal as chairman of the Atomic Power Commission. Three and a half months had elapsed between the time Congress began to consider E.R.P. and the date it was finally approved. Yet the Congress, fourteen years before, at the depth of the depression, adopted during "the first hundred days" of President Roosevelt's administration a broad program of legislation profoundly affecting the economy of the entire nation. There is nothing apparently in the congressional mechanism which makes it impossible to take speedy and effective action.

Yet in most instances the Congress moves without discrimination, apparently unable to decide between the immediate and essential and the nonimmediate and trivial. Overnight it may be persuaded that John L. Lewis or Joseph Stalin must be curbed by an impulsive legislative gesture. These expressions come only at those occasional moments when the national interest rises above local problems and under the sudden fear that the nation is in peril. The House of Representatives and, to a lesser extent, the Senate have little if any interest in the long, slow run of policy development—policy in the sense of a sustained effort and direction rather than in decision on a series of immediate choices, often made inevitable by the lack of any long-term point of view.

Nor is this confined to foreign policy. I have suggested that it is to be expected that these last three crucial years have not witnessed the development of any firm, carefully thought-out policy to guide our new position in Europe largely because our tradition has been to have no policy abroad. But the same is relatively true of our domestic policy. National domestic issues—the tariff, currency reform, budget-making—were often "logrolled" and avoided rather than clearly defined and decided. It cannot be said, to take a single instance, that the country has evolved a recognizable program for dealing with the normal conflict between labor and management except in a piecemeal and casual manner. A recurring public problem is the right of government employees to strike. Although individual executives, such as President Franklin Roosevelt and Mayor O'Dwyer in New York, have defined their attitudes, there is no recognizable national policy on this fundamental difficulty.

In the domestic field this empirical approach, which to an outside observer might appear chaotic, cumbersome, and illogical in practice, actually worked and kept together the unrelated interests of East and West, manufacturer and farmer, farmer and Wall Street, labor and industry. Generally speaking, there have been no domestic crises which were not settled under the eighteenth-century machinery of the federal system. Those who believe in its present effectiveness point, under the continuing attacks of students of government, to its success. The governments of the states and of the United States, except for the fierce interruption of the Civil War, when the federal structure proved inadequate under the pressure of irreconcilable social and economic interests, have stood firmly and peacefully since they were put into being. The federal system *has* worked.

And what is the essence of the system?

I have spoken of the balance of power between the two sovereign authorities, national and state, and of the balances between the branches within the national government. But the theory of balance of power, though psychologically revealing, cannot be separately considered in evaluating the effectiveness of the structure. The analysis must be thought of in political as well as in constitutional terms. How does it actually work, and what are the conditions on which it must operate?

That the federal method is one in which powers are separated has made it peculiarly adaptable to American problems. I do not have in mind any consideration of the doctrine of state rights, always somewhat academic, and evoked or challenged by whatever group it happened to assist or hamper in its need of the moment. But no closely integrated national organization would have suited the vast, sprawling, thinly populated continent; its people pioneer-minded, resenting authority, restless and impatient of restraint; its communications slow and far-reaching. In such a country, for such a people, as they pushed against the western barriers which beckoned and resisted, as their little communities grew necessarily as self-sustaining entities, local and provincial interests predominated. There could be no national integration. No single government could have been strong enough to rule from a central point. How could Washington in those early expanding days have afforded to the little towns a thousand miles away the simple needs of pioneer communities—school and roads, police and courts. The problems were local problems. There was absent the continuing threat of danger from the outside. These conditions made the theory of decentralization particularly applicable to the need of the American people. I have suggested in another chapter the reason why the use of checks and balances was adopted—the distrust of government authority, which the colonies had seen abused. Their thinking had been greatly influenced by Locke and Montesquieu, whose *Esprit des lois*, appearing in 1754, advocated the separation of powers as an essential "bulwark of ordered liberty." But it was not only the rejection of authority that accounted for the form the new government took. America did not begin as a nation or inherit any national tradition. Nationalism was accepted reluctantly, as a necessary arrangement for dealing with certain defined and limited subjects. The conditions of the country tended to keep it fluid and regional. It is conceivable that a national point of view might have developed in the Congress within the framework of the Constitution from a different social and economic climate. But there were no problems that could not be settled under the existing arrangements. It is significant that Bryce, after taking a look at Washington, New York, Philadelphia, Chicago, San Francisco, and New Orleans, should conclude that the United States was "the only great country in the world which has no capital."[1] He considered this a healthy condition in a democracy. But the fact illustrates the lack of any national outlook.

To understand our government, to try to estimate its strengths and its weaknesses, as we begin to use it in this immense new world role, we cannot reach valid judgment by looking solely to the written structure of the Constitution.

Just as the courts have given reality to its broad terms as they came to be applied to conflicting interests, so the action of federal officials, both in the Congress and in the executive departments, has added substance and meaning to the definition of their powers outlined in the Constitution. And this meaning may be very different from that originally intended. An example of the way in which political practice has changed the original conception is found in the application of the phrase "by and with the advice and consent of the Senate" used in relation to nominations by the President of judges and other "officers of the United States." Formally the President still nominates. But actually the nominations—at least to positions within the respective states—are almost universally made by individual senators, who can block nominations from their state on grounds of "personal privilege" without establishing any case of unfitness. And if the senators from the nominee's state are satisfied, the other senators seldom register any particular interest in the nomination. It is not their business. They have no interest in appointments outside their bailiwick. A federal judge is, in actual practice, the representative of his district or circuit, not of the nation at large, although all members of the Senate are charged with the duty of approving him. This is a striking example of the local point of view imbedded by long usage into the national body.

The Constitution requires that members of the Congress be elected from states in which they reside. Each state could have elected representatives-at-large from the whole state, who would have been less influenced by local considerations than men coming from congressional districts in which the election took place. There were thirteen representatives-at-large in the Eightieth Congress. Of these, four came from states entitled to one congressman only and three from states entitled to two. Frequently a state will have a representative-at-large where it has failed to redistrict as required by law and solves the problem by filling the places to which it is entitled by this device. With these rare exceptions, candidates invariably come from the district in which they live. Yet there is nothing in the Constitution which compels local representation, and, in view of the constitutional provision, state law could probably not require it. Our tradition has made local representation obligatory by custom.[2]

A recent illustration of the same outlook is found in the congressional handling of the "submerged oil" controversy. In 1947 the United States Supreme Court in a test case declared that the federal government had paramount rights in and power over oil under the marginal sea. Conflict over this issue between the United States and the states and municipalities formerly disposing of the oil became intense. It is probable that there are immensely valuable deposits of oil offshore on the continental shelf. One might have supposed that the government's title to the oil, thus confirmed on the highest level, would have been stubbornly supported by a majority of the Congress. On the contrary: legislation introduced by the Attorney-General and the Secretary of the Interior, providing an appropriate arrangement under which these national resources could be properly preserved and used, was sent to the Senate Committee on Interior and Insular Affairs and to the House Committee on Public Lands—and there it stuck. Senator Edward H. Moore's bill giving away the oil (and other mineral resources) to the states was referred to the judiciary committees of the House and the Senate and promptly reported favorably by the House committee and passed by the House. It was voted out of the Senate commitee by a close vote but fell by the wayside in the exodus of Congress to the national conventions. The congressional action was taken at a time of serious national emergency, with the threat of war on the horizon. The uncertainty and inadequacy of our domestic oil supply was well known and had been brought to the attention

of members of the Congress by the pleas of the Secretary of
Defense, the Attorney-General, and the Secretary of the Interior that Congress should not attempt to disturb the rights
of the United States in the marginal seas, which had been
settled by the Supreme Court. Could there be a better illustration to show that, where the two conflict, our national legislature represents local interests?

In the relation of the President to the Congress a basic development has occurred. Probably it was neither desired nor
foreseen by the Founders. The President has become the direct
representative of the people. His strength lies in this relation,
and his influence is largely determined by his ability to obtain
direct support from the people. Certainly this result was not
planned by the establishment of the electoral college, which
was intended to stand as a buffer between the unruly mob and
the Chief Executive, who was not thought of as their spokesman. The great influence of the President comes from the di-
rectness with which he appeals to the people, speaks to them
and for them, for all the people, not for any group or locality,
but as the leader of the whole country, the only national voice
in the true political sense. And in the ultimate analysis this
is the President's only strength. For Congress, if it is sufficiently united, can pass any laws it likes, appropriate any
funds it chooses, run the government irrespective of its head,
if we but look to the Constitution to discover where the
authority is written.

The President's power of national leadership, political
rather than constitutional, is a necessary corollary to the provincial and local point of view which the Congress represents.
It is not in practice a national legislative body, but in behavior and outlook a parliament not so much of states as of
local interests. The committee system, the filibuster privilege
(queer mechanisms if thought of in terms of national needs),

the practice of patronage and appointments, the endless time spent on what seems trivial—all these phenomena, which at times, and particularly now, seem curiously inept as expressions of the national will, can be understood only when we realize that to the Congress particular are far more important than general interests. This emphasis springs from the federal system, which is built on the assumption that the strength of a democracy lies where men live, grows locally in the cities and towns and villages in which their interests center, and not in any distant seat of government which can hold them by no bonds of personal reality. The community interests demand that their voices shall be heard in Washington and that they elect representatives who will speak for them.

The delays, the provincialism, and the timorous caution and prejudices so often displayed by Congress tend, I think, to obscure the value of the arrangement for a country like ours and the achievements which it has produced. Issues are fought out competitively on many levels of political authority and result in a series of compromises which settle the disputes practically, even if often temporarily. If integration and responsibility are lacking, the balance is kept and agreement achieved by innumerable arrangements from which few national interests clearly emerge. The very formlessness and fluidity of the system tend to confuse those who theoretically observe its functioning. That the two national parties do not represent vital political differences as they do in Great Britain is characteristic. If issues are avoided, so are conflicts. The difficulty of political strategists is not to settle issues but to find them. If the method tends to obscure them, it also serves to steady the government and to achieve its durability. If it results in lack of outstanding political leadership, it involves participation by the people in public affairs. If it creates indecision and planlessness, it prevents crises.

Students of the federal system have, it seems to me, over-looked these positive achievements in their analysis of the structure of the Constitution and their description of the way it works. The influence of the design of checks and balances has been exaggerated. The logic that this *constitutional* mecha-nism created the resulting irresponsibility is on the surface persuasive, particularly in the hands of such an experienced scholar and careful observer as Lord Bryce. Examined against English parliamentary government, the logic draws strength by comparison. But the comparison is misleading. The British system was gradually adopted to fit a comparatively small and compact nation with a long national tradition, a small foreign population, a society integrated physically and intellectually. The symbol of the king was essential to insure the continuity and responsibility of party government. But such an arrange-ment was not calculated to give the American people what they wanted. They did not want centralized power and admin-istration or integration on the level of national solutions.

Emphasis on local problems and the habit of presenting in Congress the district point of view have not made it impos-sible for the country to think nationally when a national crisis arose. The difficulties of attaining strong national leader-ship implemented by a united administrative outlook and backed by a broad popular choice faded into the background when the nation was at war. The federal system, with its powers scattered and divided, its state and local prejudices and pride, was believed by many Europeans to be ill fitted to the strain and challenge of war, although adequate to the minuter problems of peace. But the belief that such a democracy, with its loose and popular forms, could not act decisively when its life was threatened has been shown to be groundless in the two great wars which have recently tested democratic institu-tions. War proved that democracies could prepare effectively, act promptly, and achieve a unity of purpose and action not foreshadowed by their peace habits.

Nor has this efficiency been at the expense of democratic institutions even during the war. In 1940 the isolationists argued gloomily that preparation for war could be made only at the sacrifice of our democratic practices. Today few will suggest that victory was achieved at any such price. The war was fought by Britain and by the United States against a democratic background of a free press, open criticism, functioning courts. If the Defense of the Realm Act was resorted to in England and in Canada, its use has since the war been abandoned. In the continental United States the writ of habeas corpus was not suspended, as it was in the limited and highly vulnerable area that had been subjected to the sudden Japanese stab at Pearl Harbor. The exclusion and evacuation of persons of Japanese ancestry, most of whom were American citizens, is hard to defend. The "military necessity" did not appear until a good many weeks after Pearl Harbor and was not unrelated to the hysteria that began to sweep the country and to make life intolerable for Japanese on the West Coast. The decision was not based on any reported acts of sabotage or individual sampling. The gallantry of the Japanese-American troops, particularly in Italy, showed the country how little basis there was for the belief that they would not act as loyally as any other Americans. Today the Japanese are more accepted by and integrated into the American public than they have ever been.

But, although we sustained most of these constitutional rights under the moral pressure for a swift victory, we were not functioning as we function in time of peace. As in every modern war the executive, in substance, was given a free hand. The balance of power between the President and the Congress, unaffected as a political theory and certain to reassert itself as soon as war was over, was in effect suspended. Speed, discipline, and unity can in times of such dominating crisis be achieved, on the whole, only through executive action. The President was given substantially everything he asked for. Under the Lend-Lease statute, for instance, he could "sell, transfer title to, exchange, lease, lend, or otherwise dispose of any defense article." And what was not a "defense article"? Edward Borchard thought that the act empowered the President to make military alliances "with any foreign nation for any purpose or on any terms that he sees fit" and to place at its disposal "any part of the military establishment in the United States." The President, under the Constitution, is Commander-in-Chief. This the country and the Congress recognized. "Thus powers such as Lincoln cavalierly appropriated Congress freely granted to Roosevelt."[3]

Yet Congress did not adjourn its jurisdiction. It performed among other things a vital function in preventing much of the enormous waste that seems to be the inevitable accompaniment of war. It is pleasant now to remember the efficiency, fairness, and fearlessness of the committee headed by Senator Harry S. Truman in finding and checking a large part of that waste yet never hampering the war effort. This was in sharp contrast to the work of the Joint Committee on the Conduct of the War, appointed at the very beginning of the Civil War, on December 20, 1861, to help Congress perform its constitutional functions, which, without doubt, President Lincoln had disregarded and continued to disregard. The committee "took over partial control of military operations . . . undermined army discipline and discouraged the more capable commanders." It dictated the appointment of Edwin M. Stanton as Secretary of War and "sought to intimidate Lincoln by threatening to arouse Congress against him."[4]

But what happens in the adventurous energy of war cannot be the same as in the inertness of any peace, however critical. The normal lines of government are re-established, as indeed they should be. With every war that we have waged their robustness has been eloquently proved. The national interest, completely dominant when war is declared, falls into the background as soon as peace is resumed. The nation has needed a strong President to represent it in the crisis. That need is gone. We return to the habitual give-and-take of a parochial outlook.

But the present situation does not permit such a transition. War is over, but peace has not been restored. The crisis of war and its problems remain. There is still need for immediate decisions, for subordinating special to national considerations, for vigorous executive leadership, for an expanded and expert administration in the international field. And, even if we were not in the midst of this cold war with Russia, our new European policy and position require a more robust and flexible instrument than the federal government as we have shaped it to function. However well that system worked in the old days, it is not working very effectively at this moment. The problem is not a single emergency or the need for solving a sudden crisis. That our foreign policy during the last two years should have been presented to the public in a series of crises illustrates the American public's indifference to the creation of a unified, continuous, and thoroughly understood foreign policy of national proportions.

The country has grown together. Seven wars have added to the sense of nationalism. No longer vast spaces separate thought and action, since space has dwindled in terms of time. The problems which once were those of the single community have become more and more national needs calling for national solutions—regulation of public utilities, recognition and regulation of organized labor, social security. Yet, as the country grew more national-minded, the political tradition that the job of Congress was to look after local interests did not greatly change. Nor has Congress altered the nature of its loyalty or the sense of its responsibility. Today we are harassed with that narrow outlook as we attempt to tackle these immense world problems. We have a "government by fits and starts," with a "piecemeal, splinter approach." We bring "the vision of a parish to the politics of a planet."[5] We are faced with "the awful necessity for global thinking."[6]

The creation of national responsibility in Congress is essential if our government is to function effectively in its new sphere. This can be brought about, I believe, without changing from a federal system to a ministerial government. We must build on what we have, on a system that is ours, evolved out of our thinking and needs, incrusted with the habit of familiar practice. There is no single road to needed reform, no magic radical solution. The tree of government must grow slowly. The roots cannot be cut without danger to its flowering. Pruning must be cautious, tuned to the season. And, in considering some of the changes that have been suggested, we must always bear in mind the main objects we are after. Many suggested reforms deal with an attempt to bridge the gap between executive and legislative. But our purpose is not necessarily to draw these two functions of government together. It is *to make each responsible in its own field*. Bridging the gap may be highly useful, or it may be merely artificial and confusing.

A closer, informal co-operation between the executive and legislative is, however, highly desirable. I have already referred to the recently developed custom of the President's meeting informally with leaders of the Senate and House. This has worked well and should be continued. Dean Acheson, when he was Assistant Secretary of State, proved the value of the use of a liaison officer on a high level to keep congressional committees dealing with foreign policy informed not only of the outlines of that policy but of the constantly changing events across the world out of which it was being evolved.

During the war James V. Forrestal, when he was Secretary of the Navy, regularly arranged for members of the Naval Affairs Committee to sit in with his staff so that they could familiarize themselves at first hand with the problems under consideration. John B. Blandford, administrator of the National Housing Agency, also worked during the war in close co-operation with the Public Buildings and Grounds committees of the Senate and House.

This type of co-operation is valuable because it does not involve the confusion of responsibility which more formalized procedures may easily lead to. Where legislative and administrative functions are clearly separated, as under the federal government, any arrangement which places executive authority in the hands of members of the legislature tends to irresponsibility. Efforts by Congress to affect the administration of a statute by inserting measures which limit the necessary administrative discretion are for the same reason inadvisable. The practice of giving members of Congress executive positions, such as appointing them on international committees, raises similar difficulties of divided responsibility. Is the duty of a congressman thus appointed to follow the policy of the Administration on some question, unexpectedly arising, on which he may have taken a different view in Congress? The development of responsibility comes from a recognition within each branch of the government of the nature of its own duties and powers.

The occasional sporadic assumption by the Congress of powers outside its jurisdiction, which often follows a war in which the Executive has for the time being emerged as the center of attention, has not strengthened it as an institution. Congress must learn to abandon its immature obsession that measures proposed by the Executive are suspect and that approval of such measures automatically classifies members of Congress as "rubber stamps." Their field is not so much to initiate legislation as to criticize, to analyze, and to discuss it before adopting or rejecting it. Yet the psychological myth of the rubber stamp is continually deflecting them from their own job. If there has been a deterioration in the influence of Congress, as many believe, it is not because Congress has not the constitutional and legal power to act effectively but because it has been unwilling to use its powers, to insist on congressional discipline within its own ranks, to employ modern methods and expert advice, and, above all, to think nationally instead of provincially. "Unless Congress can," wrote E. S. Corwin five years ago, "by improving its organization and reforming some of its procedures, render itself a more consistently useful public agency, it seems likely to be reduced to the level of a badly tarnished pageant and little more."[7]

The Congress in recent years has done much to define and solidify the responsibilities of the Executive by the creation of the Civil Service System, the passage of a unified executive budget, and, recently, by charging the President, with the help of his Council of Economic Advisers, with the duty of reporting twice a year on the economic state of the country. Practice and the necessities of the situation have developed recognition of the obligation of the President to submit legislation to the Congress, just as he submits his annual budget. Yet, curiously enough, similar efforts to fix and define responsibility within the Congress have never been seriously attempted. The committee chairmen are responsible to no one, emerge to the surface on the careless lottery of seniority, and have no obligation for any national policy. Senator Robert R. Reynolds, landing by accident of seniority as chairman of the Military Affairs Committee of the Senate during the War, voted against Lend-Lease, against the transfer of Axis ships, against the extension of the draft, and against the armed-ship bill.

The La Follette–Monroney Legislative Reorganization Act of 1946 did nothing to touch the patent absurdity of filibuster in the Senate or the irresponsibility of the seniority system. Committee chairmen have no responsibility for policy, and there is no relation between policy and tenure. Whether steering committees in the respective chambers or single individuals such as the Vice-President and the Speaker, respectively, should appoint the committee chairmen is a debatable question. Because "Canonism" was grossly abused does not prove that the system under which, as Speaker, Canon flourished should have been discarded. To insure a national policy and to carry it out, a plan must be adopted under which the leaders of the party in power will have the means of deciding on a national program and the accompanying discipline to enforce it. Power must be translated into party discipline. The details of such a plan cannot be discussed in the limits of this chapter.

Basic changes in our form of government, calculated to create greater responsibility and discipline, have been frequently advocated. Our Constitution provides in Article I, Section 6: "No person holding any office under the United States shall be a member of either House during his continuance in office." It has been suggested that if this provision were repealed, cabinet officers could be drawn from Congress and, retaining their seats in Congress, would thus bring more closely together the two branches of the government. But such a device might easily have the opposite effect and would tend to confuse responsibility. It eventually fitted into the British system because both administrative and legislative power were centered in a single body, the ministry, chosen from the dominant party in Parliament. The constitutional change has never been seriously considered, but the suggestion illustrates the difficulty of imposing a procedure which has worked admirably in Great Britain but is hardly fitted to the American structure.

A more moderate change along the same lines was embodied

in Congressman Kefauver's resolution in the House during the war to permit a question period at regular intervals on the floor of the House, in which members of the Cabinet and of the government would answer questions directed to them by members of the House. It created wide discussion. Several members of President Roosevelt's Cabinet were in favor of its adoption. Similar resolutions have been suggested before. The Confederate Constitution contained such a provision. It might be an interesting experiment to adopt and would involve no fundamental change in our political structure. Yet it must be remembered that the British question period in the House chiefly serves the purpose of a sounding board both for the Government and the Opposition, even if it may have originated as a method of keeping the Parliament informed of what the Government was doing. Anything like the press conferences of the President and of the members of the Cabinet is unknown in England. If thought of as a further opportunity for the Administration to get its program known to the country, the suggestion has possibilities. It would, of course, also give members of the Congress a greater chance to heckle the Administration. It would hardly serve to bridge the gap between the two.

One suggested constitutional change would follow a pattern already implicitly accepted with increasing frequency and would achieve greater cohesiveness in our expression of foreign policy. The Constitution requires ratification of treaties by a two-thirds vote of the Senate. William Jennings Bryan is said to have remarked that it took only a majority to make war but two-thirds to make peace. In a country based on the democratic acceptance of majority rule this provision is an anomaly, with harmful implications. As Congressman Kefauver has pointed out, a treaty can be blocked by thirty-three senators representing 8 per cent of the people.[8] The record of the Senate in handling treaties of peace has not been such as would indicate the desirability of its being the sole partner of the Executive in shaping international policy. "The treaty-making process had resulted in the outright defeat of some treaties which were generally desirable, in the amendment of others frequently causing considerable irritation to the other country, and in occasional long delays."[9] Secretary of State John Hay once observed that "a treaty entering the Senate is like a bull going into the arena; no one can say just when or how the final blow will fall—but one thing is certain, it will never leave the arena alive."[10] The use of treaties, probably on account of the difficulty in obtaining a two-thirds vote in the Senate, has largely given way to the resort to executive agreements with foreign nations which are subject, like any other laws, to the approval only of a majority in both houses. There is no clear legal distinction between the two, and agreements can apparently be used interchangeably for treaties.[11] Up to 1939 our country had executed almost 2,000 international instruments, of which 1,182 were executive agreements and 799 were treaties.[12] The Charter of the United Nations was ratified by treaty; Bretton Woods, U.N.R.R.A., and the International Labor Agreement, by executive agreements. Increasingly, moreover, the fulfilment of treaties carries the necessity of substantial appropriations, a primary function of the House. If the House shared in the act of approval, it would do much to unite the two chambers and strengthen and solidify public opinion and government policy in the foreign field. A resolution for the suggested constitutional change was adopted by the House in the Seventy-ninth Session. It died in the Senate Judiciary Committee.

A third suggestion, frequently made, is to elect the President and members of both houses at the same time. This would tend to create greater responsibility and to prevent the choice of a President of a party other than that of the majority in Congress, or the election of a Senate of a different complexion from the House. The term of the President and of all legislators might well be fixed at six years. The present requirement for choosing one-third of the Senate every two years undoubtedly makes for continuity of that body. But this advantage seems to many to be outweighed by the resulting tendency to split the Senate from the House and to scatter responsibility. The election of representatives every two years is a waste of time and money and serves to dissipate the attention of the country on political matters by calling too frequently for a concentration on minor issues which, as a result, become largely alternatives of personalities.

Unity and discipline must be increased if we are to meet our new responsibilities. Changes in the operation of the Executive branch are as essential as in the operation of the Congress. Foreign policy can no longer be isolated in the State Department but concerns many other branches of the government—Defense, Commerce, Agriculture, Treasury, Interior, to mention only the departments most obviously concerned. Foreign policy can no longer be sharply separated from domestic. Each impinges on the other, and they tend to fuse. It is impossible in the long run to divide them, to isolate foreign policy by calling it "nonpartisan." Our help to Europe, the size and nature of our army, deeply affect the way we live. Therefore, the choices must be the result of debate and decision and responsible to democratic control. But the policies, once chosen, should involve, as far as possible, unified action by the officials who are to administer them. Lack of unity in the foreign field undermines the influence of the United States all over the world at this moment.

I have touched on certain suggested reforms rather to indicate the direction they might take than to propose a solution. If, as I believe, we shall not come to our own until we learn to think nationally *and* internationally, no changes in our form of government, however advisable, will cure our weakness. But they can make it easier for a new form of thinking to operate. Ultimately, however, it is not a matter of the mechanics of the government but of the understanding and will of the people.

X

CONCLUSION

✧

I HAVE tried to suggest in the preceding chapters some of the problems which confront the United States as she stands at this moment in the center of the world. We have come a very long way since the days when all foreign alliances were considered entangling. Two world wars wakened us to a sense of reality. The immense influence of Great Britain had sustained a world economy by keeping world trade open and relatively free. Her military power had policed the competition of national aggression. Yet for almost a half-century she has been losing her commanding industrial position, as Brooks Adams realized as far back as 1900. "From Waterloo down to 1899," he wrote, "Great Britain acted as a sort of balance wheel to human society, she operated as the containing force of civilization. . . . England has stood aside, and as she has effaced herself Russia has dilated. . . . Apparently America must more or less completely assume the place once held by England."[1] We began to realize that we must fill that place when we saw on the Eastern Hemisphere the vacuum that had been slowly created under the shadow of the Soviet bear.

The physical resources, the industrial might, a navy that no nation can approach, incalculable reserves of credit, unsurpassed technical ability—all these are centered in the United States. Can we use this power, greater than has ever before been concentrated in the hands of a single nation, to hold the world together? Can we accept the responsibility that goes with our might, the duty to achieve and to sustain the peace of the world? Are we still in "the full tide of successful experiment"? Is this government now, as Thomas Jefferson said of it nearly a hundred and fifty years ago, the "world's best hope"?

For until the great powers transfer to an international organization the actual strength of their pooled resources there can be no peace unless that peace is achieved, as Britain once achieved it, by the wise and skilful use of national prestige, resting on national force. Until the struggle is ended which day to day goes on between the Soviet Union and her satellites and the United States and those nations which are grouped about her, the traditionally historic effort of Russia to expand and the new attempt of America to contain this thrust of imperialism and to rebuild the saner forces of national recovery—until that contest is determined or abandoned on terms that both nations will accept, the United Nations can have but a paper life, without breath of immediate hope or blood of vitality or action.

Today we face this heroic task of peace, infinitely more complex than the waging of a war, without a clearly defined policy, political or strategic, or more than the negative outline of one; with a thin experience, lacking experts to carry out whatever course we finally choose; with a faltering and timorous Congress, unwilling to follow the leadership of the President and Secretary of State until they have pawed over the figures for months to show the country how careful they can be; with the creaking and antiquated machinery of the federal government and its ineffable absurdities of filibuster and seniority rule; these United States, confused and uncertain, the greatest power in the world, the richest, unscarred by the war, doubted, envied, feared, hated, admired by the other nations. . . .

We cannot ignore our power. How shall we use it?

The sources of our weakness lie in our own hearts and minds. That is not to belittle the qualities of our outlook—our friendliness, our hard good sense in handling concrete problems, our generosity, tested again and again by our quick response to the suffering of others. But these virtues are too often accompanied by an enveloping complacency which springs from immature satisfaction with our own material achievements. We tend to live, as it were, by a series of unrelated experiments, in the immediate day of the present, with little sense of the overlap of the past. We have no historical perspective. Thirty-five years ago, when our problems were far less difficult than they are now, Lawrence Lowell wrote: "Our people have an horizon so limited, a knowledge of the past so small, a self-confidence so sublime, a conviction that they are altogether better than their fathers so profound, that they hardly realize the difficulty of their task."[2]

As I said in the Introduction, an immediate question that confronts us is whether the free-enterprise system of the United States can be made to work in harmony with the Socialist economies of western Europe. The growth of time should have taught us that the differences are less than most of us believe. What is "socialism" today becomes an accepted practice of "free enterprise" tomorrow. The rigid classification is meaningless in a world where no country has a free economy in any exact sense, where co-operative efforts have taken the place of personal interests, where eighteenth- and early nineteenth-century individualism has given way to a highly organized life. The differences between free enterprise and socialism are, more and more, differences of degree.

Yet, judged by the public pronouncements of their trade associations, a majority of American businessmen, like the "philosophers of the old school," still regard any government activity related to business "as an artificial interference with the wisdom of Providence made manifest in the distribution of wealth according to merit under natural law."[3]

In practice we have long since ceased to relate these doctrinaire rationalizations to the workings of our own government. This is hardly the time to apply them to the governments of our new partners in western Europe.

We have lived at peace; we have traded with Socialist countries before. There is no reason why we cannot continue to do so. There is every reason why we must. I have elaborated at some length in a previous chapter the theme that totalitarian countries are in no true sense Socialist—that they are, in fact, as much opposed to socialism as to democracy. We have gone to war with three of them—Japan, Germany, Italy—when they became strong enough to challenge the freedom of the rest of the world. The struggle in which we are involved is not new. It is not a conflict between two divergent economic systems. It is the continued resistance of free men and of independent nations to the usurping aggression of a world dictator.

Resistance, however, is but a negative role, not calculated to enlist and to hold the weary hearts of men. We must strive to re-create a new world, as well as to bring into balance the old one. History has taught people to believe that national power means imperialism. We can become the most powerful imperial empire the world has ever known and exploit weaker nations under the pious excuse of "the white man's burden." We have not been free from adventures of domination in the past. "The annexation of Porto Rico," the Beards wrote, "and absorption of Cuba . . . had been merely a prelude to the transformation of the Gulf of Mexico and the Caribbean into an inland sea of the United States."[4] But our tradition and instincts, our geographical and political isolation, have not favored a policy of colonial expansion. We have not exploited Cuba or the Philippines or sought to plant colonies in the Pacific. The Monroe Doctrine has not been a cloak for Yankee imperialism. Our most recent policy in the Mediterranean has led to no attempts to control independent powers and make them subservient to our own. On the contrary, we are engaged in building and sustaining the independence of other nations and their industrial recovery. Such a program can be turned to the backward places of the earth, not to establish spheres of influence, or to develop a colonial status, but to introduce the benefits of modern industry and science, and the free democratic institutions which are their cultural counterpart.

Time runs short. The history of that word "democracy" is now to be enacted.

NOTES

✢

INTRODUCTION

1. *Economist* (London), February 7, 1948.
2. George Santayana, *Character and Opinion in the United States* (New York: Charles Scribner's Sons, 1921), p. 14.

CHAPTER I

1. *America's Needs and Resources* (New York: Twentieth Century Fund, 1947), pp. 646–47.
2. *Saturday Review of Literature*, July 5, 1947.
3. *America's Needs and Resources*, pp. 647, 142, 163, 164, 413.
4. *Ibid.*, pp. 574 and 597.
5. Samuel E. Morison, *The Oxford History of the United States* (New York: Oxford University Press, 1927), I, 6, 46, 45, 41.
6. *Ibid.*, II, 118.
7. *Democracy in America* (New York: Alfred A. Knopf, 1945), I, 131, 234.
8. *The American Commonwealth* (New York: Macmillan Co., 1908), I, 71, 107, 343; II, 332, 371, 523, 524, 522. Copyright, 1893, by Macmillan and Company and used with their permission. References will be made to the 1908 edition unless otherwise indicated.
9. Radio Address from Paris, Department of State, September 8, 1947, No. 724.
10. *New York Times*, May 20, 1948.
11. Charles A. and Mary R. Beard, *The Rise of American Civilization* (New York: Macmillan Co., 1927), II, 788. Copyright, 1927, 1930, and 1933, by The Macmillan Company and used with their permission.
12. *New York Times*, November 4, 1947.

13. 90 Nassau Street, Princeton, N.J.

14. President's Air Policy Commission, *Survival in the Air Age* (Washington, D.C.: Government Printing Office, January 1, 1948), pp. 4, 7, 14, 15, 20. (Italics added.)

15. Walter Lippmann, *U.S. Foreign Policy: Shield of the Republic* (Boston: Little, Brown & Co., 1943), p. 17. Copyright, 1943, by Little, Brown and Company and The Atlantic Monthly Press. Canning had indicated to the American minister, Richard Rush, that he believed that no "concert in action" would be necessary, because the "moral effect" would be "founded upon the large share of the maritime power of the world which Great Britain and the United States shared between them, and the consequent influence which the knowledge that they held a common opinion . . . could not fail to produce upon the rest of the world" (J. Reuben Clark, *Memorandum on the Monroe Doctrine* [Department of State Pub. 37, December 17, 1928 (Washington, D.C.: Government Printing Office, 1930)]).

16. Quoted by Morison, *op. cit.*, I, 364.

17. Beard and Beard, *op. cit.*, II, 611.

18. *Op. cit.*, p. 7.

19. Barbara Ward, "Britain in the Shadow," *Harper's Magazine*, November, 1947.

20. *Op. cit.*, I, 434. (Italics added.)

CHAPTER II

1. *The Congress of Vienna* (London: Constable & Co., 1946).

2. Quoted by Charles A. and Mary R. Beard, *The Rise of American Civilization*, II, 612.

3. *Ibid.*, p. 496.

4. *European Recovery and American Aid: A Report by the President's Committee on Foreign Aid* (Washington, D.C.: Government Printing Office, November 7, 1947), pp. 21–22.

5. *"To Secure These Rights": The Report of the President's Committee on Civil Rights* (Washington, D.C.: Government Printing Office, 1947), p. 49.

6. *Department of State Bulletin*, XI, No. 277 (October 15, 1944), 401.

7. *The Development of the Foreign Reconstruction Policy of the United*

States, March–July, 1947 (Department of State Pub. 2912 [Washington, D.C.: Government Printing Office, 1947]).

8. James F. Byrnes, *Speaking Frankly* (New York: Harper & Bros., 1947), pp. 299–300.

9. "Balance of Power," *Life*, September 22, 1947.

10. *Ibid.* What I have said here is, in substance, a summary of this interesting article.

11. *New York Times*, December 14, 1947.

12. Mr. Justice Holmes, dissenting in *Tyson* v. *Banton*, 273 U.S. 418, 445 (1926).

13. *The Development of the Foreign Reconstruction Policy of the United States.*

14. "The Challenge to Americans," *Foreign Affairs*, October, 1947.

15. *Complete Prose Works* (New York: D. Appleton & Co., 1908), p. 222.

CHAPTER III

1. Concurring opinion in *Whitney* v. *California*, 274 U.S. 357, 372 (1927); address before the New Century Club, Boston, April 6, 1915. Cf. Alfred Lief, *The Brandeis Guide to the Modern World* (Boston: Little, Brown & Co., 1941), p. 72.

2. *New York Times*, February 5, 1947.

3. *Oriental View of American Civilization*, quoted in Henry Steele Commager (ed.), *America in Perspective* (New York: Random House, 1947), pp. 334–36. By permission of No Yong-Park.

4. Commager (ed.), *op. cit.*, pp. 262, 267–68.

5. *Ibid.*, p. 13.

6. *Democracy in America*, II, 129, 318–19. It should be remembered that these remarks were addressed to democratic governments in general, not to the United States in particular.

7. *The American Commonwealth*, II, 819, 825.

8. See Commager (ed.), *op. cit.*

9. *"To Secure These Rights,"* p. 4.

10. R. H. Tawney, *Equality* (New York: Harcourt, Brace & Co., 1929), p. 114. By permission of George Allen & Unwin, Ltd., the British publisher. I am indebted to this brilliant study for much that I say here.

11. *The Rise of American Civilization*, II, 53.

12. Tawney, *op. cit.*, p. 92.

13. *"To Secure These Rights,"* p. 4.

14. *Public Opinion and Popular Government* (London: Longmans, Green & Co., 1913), p. 131. Copyright, 1913, by Longmans, Green and Company.

CHAPTER IV

1. Sir Henry Maine, *Popular Government* (New York: Henry Holt & Co., 1886), p. 185.

2. Gaillard Hunt and James Brown Scott (eds.), *The Debates in the Federal Convention of 1787 Which Framed the Constitution of the United States of America, Reported by James Madison: International Edition* (New York: Oxford University Press, 1920), pp. 31, 32, 33, and 65.

3. Samuel E. Morison, *The Oxford History of the United States*, I, 92.

4. A. Lawrence Lowell, *Public Opinion and Popular Government*, pp. 105 and 109.

5. George B. Galloway, *Congress at the Crossroads* (New York: Thomas Y. Crowell Co., 1946), p. 285.

6. *Democracy in America*, I, 183.

7. James Bryce, *The American Commonwealth*, II, 349.

8. Quoted in Henry Steele Commager (ed.), *America in Perspective* (New York: Random House, 1947), pp. 315, 317, 319. From Richard Müller-Freinfels, *The Mysteries of the Soul* (London: George Allen & Unwin, Ltd., 1927). By permission of Allen & Unwin.

9. Lowell, *op. cit.*, pp. 244–45.

10. *Ibid.*; p. 303.

11. *The American People* (New York: W. W. Norton & Co., Inc., 1948), p. 225. By permission of W. W. Norton and Company, Inc. Copyright, 1948, by Geoffrey Gorer.

12. *Investigation of the National Defense Program* (Section 1, Report No. 10, Part 15 [78th Cong., 2d sess. (Washington, D.C.: Government Printing Office, 1943)]), p. 23.

CHAPTER V

1. James Bryce, *The American Commonwealth*, I, 306.

2. *Ibid.*, p. 307.

3. Felix Frankfurter, *Law and Politics* (New York: Harcourt, Brace & Co., 1939), p. 242.

4. H. L. Mencken, *A New Dictionary of Quotations* (New York: Alfred A. Knopf, 1942), p. 275.

5. S. E. Morison, *The Oxford History of the United States*, II, 371.

6. *Op. cit.*, II, 544.

7. Charles A. and Mary R. Beard, *The Rise of American Civilization*, II, 591.

8. *Op. cit.*, II, 176.

9. Beard and Beard, *op. cit.*, I, 749–51.

10. *Ibid.*, II, 596.

11. *Investigation of the Tennessee Valley Authority* (76th Cong., 1st sess.; Senate Doc. No. 56 [Washington, D.C.: Government Printing Office, 1939]), p. 89.

12. George W. Stocking and Myron W. Watkins, *Cartels in Action* (New York: Twentieth Century Fund, 1946), pp. 12–13.

13. *New York Times*, August 20, 1947.

14. Morison, *op. cit.*, I, 6.

15. *New York Times*, October 23, 1947.

16. Beard and Beard, *op. cit.*, II, 539–40.

17. *Abrams* v. *United States*, 250 U.S. 616, 624 (1919).

18. Lewis L. Lorwin, *Postwar Plans of the United Nations* (New York: Twentieth Century Fund, 1943), p. 35.

CHAPTER VI

1. James Bryce, *The American Commonwealth*, II, 144; 1937 ed., p. 148. Cf. Spencer D. Albright, *The American Ballot* (Washington, D.C.: American Council of Public Affairs, 1942).

2. *"To Secure These Rights,"* p. 51.

3. *Ibid.*, pp. 87, viii, ix, 20, and 139.

4. Robert K. Carr, *Federal Protection of Civil Rights: Quest for a Sword* (Ithaca, N.Y.: Cornell University Press, 1947), pp. 3, 5, 1, 193.

5. "A World Bill of Rights," *Social Service Review*, XXI (December, 1947), 440.

6. *The American People*, p. 224. Reprinted by permission of W. W. Norton Company, Inc. Copyright, 1948, by Geoffrey Gorer.

7. *Constitution of the Union of Soviet Socialist Republics* (Moscow:

Co-operative Publishing Society of Foreign Workers in the U.S.S.R., 1936), chap. x.

8. United States Department of State, *Documents and State Papers*, Vol. I, No. 1 (April, 1948). See particularly Arts. 32, 36, 71, 75, and 139.

9. *New York Times*, June 19, 1948.

CHAPTER VII

1. *New York Times*, November 21, 1947.

2. *Lochner* v. *New York*, 198 U.S. 45, 74 (1904).

3. Mr. Justice Brandeis dissenting in *New State Ice Co.* v. *Liebmann*, 285 U.S. 262, 305 (1932); *Guillotte* v. *New Orleans*, 12 La. Ann. 432 (1857); *Mobile* v. *Yuille*, 3 Ala. 137 (1841); 33 *Harv. L. Rev.* 838, 839.

4. *New York Times*, December 4, 1947.

5. *Ibid.*, November 18, 1947.

6. *Ibid.*

7. *Ibid.*, December 11, 1947.

8. James Harrington, *The Commonwealth of Oceana* (1658); H. L. Mencken, *A New Dictionary of Quotations*, p. 901.

9. *New York Times*, December 29, 1947.

10. *Ibid.*, December 30, 1947.

11. Harold E. Stassen, *Where I Stand* (New York: Doubleday & Co., Inc., 1947), p. 205.

12. *New York Times Magazine*, November 16, 1947.

13. *New York Times*, November 6, 1947.

14. *Philadelphia Bulletin*, November 14, 1947.

15. National Association of Manufacturers press releases for these two days.

16. *New York Times*, January 23, 1948.

17. Grant S. McClellan, "Britain's Crisis and American Aid," *Foreign Policy Reports*, Vol. XXIII, No. 20 (January 1, 1948).

18. *European Recovery and American Aid*, pp. 4 and 5.

19. "The Challenge to Americans," *Foreign Affairs*, October, 1947.

20. *New York Times*, November 11, 1947.

21. *Ibid.*, May 13, 1948.

22. *Ibid.*, December 24, 1947.

23. *Ibid.*, November 3, 1947.

24. "The Industrial Charter" (Brighton: Conservative and Unionist Central Office, May, 1947).

25. *New York Times*, October 6, 1947.

CHAPTER VIII

1. *Washington Post*, November 25, 1947. (Italics added.)

2. Arthur Koestler, *The Yogi and the Commissar* (New York: Macmillan Co., 1946), p. 182. Copyright, 1945, by Arthur Koestler. Used by permission of The Macmillan Company.

3. *The Russian Enigma* (New York: Charles Scribner's Sons, 1943), p. 159.

4. Grant S. McClellan, "Britain's Crisis and American Aid," *Foreign Policy Reports*, Vol. XXIII (January 1, 1948).

5. For the text of the judgment see 6 *Federal Rules Decisions*, No. 2 (December, 1946), pp. 69, 81.

6. Louis P. Lochner (ed.), *The Goebbels Diaries* (New York: Doubleday & Co., Inc., 1948), pp. 127, 133. (Italics added.)

7. *New York Times*, December 23, 1947.

8. *Constitution of the Union of Soviet Socialist Republics*, chaps. ix and x. Cf. *Communism in Action*, prepared under the direction of Representative Everett M. Dirksen (House Doc. No. 754 [Washington, D.C.: Government Printing Office, 1946]), p. 139.

9. *New York Times*, October 10, 1947.

10. *New York Times Magazine*, January 18, 1948.

11. *Op. cit.*, p. 116.

12. "Appraisals of Russian Economic Statistics," *Review of Economic Statistics*, November, 1947.

13. Quoted by Chamberlin, *op. cit.*, p. 98.

14. Koestler, *op. cit.*, p. 151.

15. Chamberlin, *op. cit.*, p. 109.

16. Koestler, *op. cit.*, p. 152.

17. David I. Dallin, *The Real Soviet Russia* (New Haven: Yale University Press, 1944), p. 116. (Italics added.)

18. Dirksen, *op. cit.*, pp. 35, 45, 43.

19. Koestler, *op. cit.*, p. 159.

20. Dirksen, *op. cit.*, p. 30.

21. Koestler, *op. cit.*, p. 156.

22. Dirksen, *op. cit.*, pp. 30 and 44.

23. Chamberlin, *op. cit.*, pp. 160–62; Koestler, *op. cit.*, pp. 160, 162, 163.

24. Dirksen, *op. cit.*, p. 39.

25. 6 *Federal Rules Decisions*, No. 2, p. 81.

26. Koestler, *op. cit.*, pp. 166–74, 179.

27. *New York Times*, January 13, 1948.

28. Chamberlin, *op. cit.*, p. 146.

29. Dirksen, *op. cit.*, p. 56.

30. Chamberlin, *op. cit.*, p. 142.

31. January 17, 1948.

32. Walter Lippmann, *The Good Society* (Boston: Little, Brown & Co., 1937), p. 67. Copyright, 1937, by Little, Brown and Company and The Atlantic Monthly Press.

33. Henry Hazlitt, *Will Dollars Save the World?* (New York: D. Appleton–Century Co., Inc., 1947), p. 61. Copyright, 1947, by Henry Hazlitt.

34. *New York Times*, July 26, 1948.

35. *The Meaning of Treason* (New York: Viking Press, 1947), p. 307.

CHAPTER IX

1. James Bryce, *The American Commonwealth*, II, 791.

2. Robert Luce, *Legislative Assemblies* (Boston: Houghton Mifflin Co., 1924), pp. 223–25.

3. Wilfred E. Binkley, *President and Congress* (New York: Alfred A. Knopf, 1947), p. 265.

4. *Ibid.*, p. 115.

5. George G. Galloway, *Congress at the Crossroads* (New York: Thomas Y. Crowell Co., 1946), pp. 223, 195, 119.

6. Estes Kefauver and Jack Levin, *A Twentieth-Century Congress* (New York: Duell, Sloan & Pearce, 1947), p. 7. Copyright, 1947, by Essential Books.

7. Quoted in Binkley, *op. cit.*, p. 267.

8. Kefauver and Levin, *op. cit.*, p. 82.

9. Quincy Wright, "The United States and International Agreements," *American Journal of International Law*, July, 1944, p. 353.

10. Kefauver and Levin, *op. cit.*, p. 85.

11. Wright, *op. cit.*, p. 355.

12. Kefauver and Levin, *op. cit.*, p. 89.

CHAPTER X

1. *America's Economic Supremacy* (reprint; New York: Harper & Bros., 1947), pp. 173 and 174.

2. *Public Opinion and Popular Government*, p. 262.

3. Charles A. and Mary R. Beard, *The Rise of American Civilization*, II, 580.

4. *Ibid.*, p. 501.

F°G5·B47